Breaking the Silence

A Play

Stephen Poliakoff

Samuel French – London
New York – Sydney – Toronto – Hollywood

BREAKING THE SILENCE

First produced by the Royal Shakespeare Company at the Pit, Barbican Theatre, on 31st October, 1984, with the following cast of characters:

Polya	Juliet Stevenson
Master Alexander (Sasha)	Jason Lake
Eugenia Pesiakoff	Gemma Jones
Alexei Verkoff	John Kane
Nikolai Pesiakoff	Daniel Massey
Guard 1	Richard Garnett
Guard 2	Campbell Morrison

Directed by Ron Daniels
Designed by Alison Chitty

Subsequently presented by Frank and Woji Gero, Frederick Zollo, William Suter and Harold Thau at the Mermaid Theatre, London, on 28th May, 1985, with the following cast:

Polya	Jenny Agutter
Master Alexander (Sasha)	Edward Rawle-Hicks
Eugenia Pesiakoff	Gemma Jones
Alexei Verkoff	John Kane
Nikolai Pesiakoff	Alan Howard
Guard 1	Paul Rattee
Guard 2	Christopher Saul

Directed by Ron Daniels
Designed by Alison Chitty

The action of the play takes place in a railway carriage in Russia

Time—1920 and 1924

ACT I 1920
Scene 1 100 miles North of Moscow
Scene 2 1,000 miles North of Moscow
Scene 3 100 miles North of Moscow
Scene 4 The same

ACT II 1924
Scene 1 Moscow Railway Shunting Yards
Scene 2 The same
Scene 3 The Border

ACT I*

SCENE 1

A huge imperial-style railway carriage, filling the whole of the stage. 100 miles north of Moscow

Rich dark wood, a table, chairs set against the walls, at one end a splendid couch elaborately decorated, which has been converted into a bed, at the other end two bunks covered in pale velvet counterpanes, a white stove built into the wall, ornamental woodwork and lamps. Over the beds and on parts of the floor, there is a coating of dirt, dust, a few bloodstains, some animal droppings, smudging the atmosphere of magnificence in the carriage. The pale bed coverings are especially filthy. The blinds across the windows are also stained yellow and black

There is the sound of people struggling with the door, then it opens, throwing a little light inside, and Polya and Sasha move into the darkened carriage

Polya is in her early thirties, dressed in a maid's dress, black with a white bow in her hair. Sasha at the start of the action is in his early teens, but looks young for his age, immaculately dressed in a velvet suit. For a second Polya stands in the doorway staring into the darkened carriage, then she moves in, pulling up the blinds to let in light. She is carrying two highly polished pigskin suitcases. Sasha is only carrying some rather grubby toy stuffed animal

Polya Stay there Master Alexander—(*as she moves into the darkened carriage alone*)—and don't touch, you understand, don't touch anything.

She pulls up the blinds to reveal the state of the carriage, as light floods in

They certainly haven't bothered to clean it for your father.

Sasha (*in the doorway*) What an extraordinary carriage Polya . . . What was it used for?

Polya Don't come in! I told you, stay there by the door until I know it's safe for you . . . there might be something here that can harm you. Something that could give you a disease. (*She moves away from the windows into the carriage, as an advanced guard*) Whatever this smell is . . . I don't think the original passengers would have smelled like that.

Sasha (*pointing at the floor*) What are those?

Polya Animal droppings—they must have used it for transporting livestock recently. That's why the beds have been chewed . . .

Sasha (*moving a little deeper into the carriage*) They can't really mean this Polya! . . . It needs hosing down before it's nearly ready for Papa. You must have misunderstood. I am sure they only intend to show it to him . . .

---

*N.B. Paragraph 3 on page ii of this Acting Edition regarding photocopying and video-recording should be carefully read.

Polya (*swinging round, loudly*) Did I say it was safe for you to come in? No.

Sasha stops

> You can stay there now, but don't move. (*She turns back to her beds*) Now don't you start causing me trouble, they haven't allowed me any time to make it fit for the master. (*She is rolling up the counterpane*) The filth that is here ... he will never sleep in sheets like this, not under any circumstances, nobody could make him. I don't know how I am going to keep my uniform clean.

By removing the stained counterpanes, the carriage is already looking less stained

Sasha (*as Polya bustles around*) Everything is such a hurry now—suddenly the news that Papa has to leave home, having to pack his things up in a few hours, I am sure we dropped something on the way here ... Papa will demand compensation I expect.

Polya If I can get these out of the way before they come, there must be at least one clean place for the master—thank God I managed to bring some extra blankets for him.

Sasha What are these holes? (*He is running his hand along the side of the carriage*) Polya, everywhere here is covered in small holes.

Polya What do you think they are! Bullet holes of course. (*She points above the windows*) There's some marks up there too ... it looks as if it was shelled.

Sasha They must be going to redecorate it. (*Exploring the carriage*) What are these red stains here Polya? It's splashed all over here, it can't be what I think it is Polya, (*he pauses*) it's not blood is it?

Polya Yes, it's blood. The goats they kept, they probably slaughtered them in here as well.

She looks up to see Sasha is suddenly very animated, searching all the corners of the carriage

> What on earth are you doing? I told you not to touch anything.

Sasha I was just seeing if there was any—(*he stops and faces her*)—even the smallest piece of ... (*suddenly shouting*) ... FOOD had been left anywhere. (*He picks up a glass jar, with one onion at the bottom, and tries to unscrew the top which is very stiff*) There's an onion here! I'm so—I'm so hungry Polya. (*Suddenly letting his body go limp and falling into her arms*) I'm going to die.

Polya Stand up. (*Pulling her body up*) Come on stand up. (*Firmly*) listen now Alexander Nikolaivitch, don't you *dare* show it when they come—you're not going to let the Commissar of Labour see the slightest sign you understand. You don't want to let your father down. (*Holding him*) Come on. You can manage ... you can get through.

Sasha I am going to die before the end of the day, I can feel it.

Polya Well wait till then at least—(*turning back to the bed*)—the master will see to everything, *remember* that.

Eugenia enters. A fine-looking woman about forty. She has a nervous, shy manner. She is dressed in an exquisite and expensive long summer dress

Eugenia I didn't imagine it would look like this. (*Looking around*) This is rather sordid isn't it? These beds ... (*She touches them*) What a place!

Polya Madame, careful where you move. If you want to sit, I think this space is safe.

Eugenia (*anxiously*) I am not sure the master is expecting this ... have you all his clothes prepared? (*She gets up immediately and moves over*) Is this all there is left? All that remains of his wardrobe. It looks so little suddenly.

Polya We've still got all his English shoes. (*She pulls them out of the suitcase*)

Eugenia As far as possible everything must go in its proper place. (*She turns suddenly*) Do we look all right, Polya, not too pale, tell me honestly—we don't seem disgracefully pale do we?

Polya No madame.

Eugenia (*smiling*) It doesn't look as if I'm about to collapse at any moment I hope. (*She tries to open the jar with the onion*)

Polya (*indicating the jar*) It won't open, Madame.

Eugenia (*embarrassed, puting the jar down*) I never used to eat onions, anyway.

Sasha is holding his stomach leaning against the wall of the carriage

Sasha! Don't do that.

Verkoff comes into the carriage, a powerful burly man, utilitarian clothes, a man in his 40s, working-class accent. He is full of a sudden, unpredictable energy, mercurial manner. He carries a bag which he throws on the floor

Verkoff We are here! (*He turns and looks behind him*) Where is he? He was right behind me. What are you doing out there Nikolai Semenovitch? (*Loudly*) Get in here! My time is limited.

Nikolai is in the doorway

What on earth are you looking so reluctant for? Come on in. Take the plunge.

Nikolai is framed in the doorway. He is an imposing figure in his late forties or early fifties, wearing a truly splendid fur coat, though it is summer, gleaming polished shoes, and a fine English suit. His manner is extremely authoritative and dignified, though there is a very distinctive charm and lightness of touch even when he's being arrogant. Everything about him is redolent of an old world, upper middle-class man. The only thing he is carrying is a medium-sized mahogany box

Nikolai (*staring into the carriage*) My God ...

Verkoff (*moving round, touching everything*) What's the matter—you should feel at home here! Gold-topped taps—what looks like a German commode, right size for one anyway—imperial furniture.

Verkoff, pulling at the bunks, suddenly jumps on to the lower bunk, scattering dried feathers

A little dirty perhaps, but you could sleep through anything in this—(*a sharp smile*)—and you may *need* to.

Nikolai (*moving into the carriage, calmly*) Is there anywhere in this carriage that it is possible to sit?

Eugenia (*nervously*) Here ...

As Nikolai sits next to Eugenia, Verkoff has resumed roaming the carriage

Verkoff (*suddenly pointing at Sasha*) The boy looks terrified, you'll have to teach him not to look at people like that—(*he smiles*)—they could feel unappreciated.

Nikolai He is just a little surprised like all of us.

Verkoff So I can see! (*He turns*) You do understand Nikolai Semenovitch what is happening to you—(*Stopping and staring at him*) You are now a Government employee with all the responsibility that entails. You will take up the position—as of now (*clicking his fingers*) of Telephone Surveyor of the Northern Railway.

Nikolai (*looking up*) Telephone Surveyor?

Verkoff Yes, Surveyor. (*Pulling at pieces of the carriage, touching every-thing*) You don't like it? He doesn't like that title, then we can change it ... (*a sharp smile*) ... the only thing that can be changed ... Telephone Examiner is acceptable ... you have just become the first Telephone Examiner of the Northern District.

Silence

Nikolai I thank you for this unexpected offer, for making the journey specially.

Verkoff Which I haven't ...

Nikolai But of course it is completely out of the question, I will have to refuse.

Pause

Verkoff (*loudly*) You will have to refuse!

Nikolai (*calmly*) I am much too busy I'm afraid.

Verkoff Too busy, I don't believe this! You have just been sitting here in the country ... this is not an *offer*, Nikolai Semenovitch, there is no refusal possible. You are MADE Telephone Examiner, it has been decided, once you've been selected and put on board, there is no alternative, no argument—the matter is completely closed.

Nikolai (*calmly*) I see. (*After a pause*) I will still have to refuse.

Verkoff I don't think we understand each other, Nikolai Semenovitch. I am a busy man and have very little time.

Nikolai (*incisive tones*) But I have told you what I need. I made repeated representations to you and your staff, and was made to wait on more than one occasion, sitting on the floor outside your door. I travelled no fewer than six times to your office, I made it absolutely clear what I had to have.

Verkoff (*with a slight smile*) Remind me what this was.

Nikolai It was a very modest request, the bare minimum in fact. A room of my own in Moscow, apart from living quarters for my family of course, for the sake of argument say five rooms, a proper staff of my own prepared to work, and sufficient time free of interruption and official interference—to think.

Verkoff (*incredulously*) To think!

Nikolai Of course. I have some specific ideas of the greatest importance, I thought I gave your advisers all the indications they needed. And I have to admit I fail to see what the problem is, you have my word for it that you will not be wasting your time. What more do you need?

Verkoff Nikolai Semenovitch——

Nikolai (*carrying straight on*) Furthermore, you gave us absolutely no warning that this was about to happen, you suddenly inform us that you will be taking over our whole house.

Verkoff (*ebullient*) Warning! You don't get any warning, you know about it when it happens to you.

Nikolai (*in an amazed tone*) And why me? How was I chosen? I'm afraid I am not the right person to watch telephone poles being erected.

Eugenia (*nervously*) My husband means that he——

Nikolai (*calmly*) In the chaos of a new filing system it is obvious there must have been a mistake, stumbling on me to be Telephone Surveyor is not a rational act, do I look a likely candidate? It is not disgrace to admit there has been an error and have it rectified—immediately.

Verkoff (*with a mercurial smile*) There is no possibility of an error I assure you, *I* made the decision personally—you were after all supposedly head of your family's engineering firm were you not? How many times you were ever there is another question of course.

Nikolai We did not concern ourselves with telephone poles.

Verkoff Don't try to test my patience—it can have dramatic results. (*He points at the women and Sasha*) You three will pack up *all* your belongings (*a slight smile*) in that sizeable house of yours, which I am told the army needs. Be ready to move immediately he returns.

Eugenia (*very nervously*) Move where, comrade?

Verkoff You will all live in here, of course.

Nikolai (*after a momentary pause*) That is clearly impossible. In no circumstances can I allow my wife to live inside here.

Verkoff (*loudly, very animated*) Listen to him! My God, there have been people dying all along the line, whole households starving, wiped out, and he complains about being here. (*His bulky shape moves about the carriage, his hand jabbing out*) I have many urgent calls to make before the light goes ... NOW, this is where things get serious. There are certain things you have to know and do, so you better be listening—(*he suddenly swings round and shouts*)—are you comrade?

Nikolai looks up in surprise

Because these matter.

Nikolai is impassive

Eugenia Of course ... we do realize.

Verkoff (*staring at them*) GUNS—(*he pauses*)—there must be no guns of any sort kept here. You are civilians—as you know, new laws have been passed—any civilian found with firearms or explosives will be executed. (*A sudden sharp smile*) If you have any, this is not a time to be shy, give them to me and no action will be taken.

Nikolai That is the law? I had no idea.

Verkoff Are you going to give them to me? I urge you to take this seriously comrade, otherwise the consequences for you and your family could be disastrous.

Silence

Nikolai Quite. Thank you for your warning. There is no need to labour the point. What is next?

Verkoff You are required to keep ledgers, official records that must be up to date. The exact times and places, and the progress you find. I am giving you ten thousand roubles. (*He throws the money which is in a bag on the floor of the carriage, at Nikolai's feet*) This will be used for railways business only, the bonus scheme we have in operation for rewarding good work, all the usual things.

Nikolai What is usual for a Telephone Examiner?

Verkoff You will take this first trip, which will be a gruelling one, and then you will wait in a siding for further instructions.

Nikolai In a *siding*? That can't be necessary . . .

Verkoff (*ignoring this*) If you ever wish to summon a locomotive in an emergency, you will walk the eighteen miles down the line and use the railway telephone to the depot. (*He points suddenly at Eugenia*) What's your name?

Eugenia (*nervously glancing about her*) My name . . . you mean me? It's Eugenia Michailovna.

Verkoff (*staring straight at her*) You think he's been listening Eugenia Michailovna? You ought to make him, people have been turned off trains before now, in the North, and made to walk the thousand miles home. (*Lightly*) I wonder how he'd manage.

Nikolai is sitting impassive in his fur coat

(*Suddenly turning towards Polya*) And *you*, what's your name? What is your position here?

Polya I am the second chamber maid, comrade—I mean I *was* in Moscow, there was me and Anya . . . (*suddenly nervous*) . . . and Luiba who cooked. (*She looks away embarrassed*) I . . . I was going to be married to the porter of an apartment block in Moscow but we lost touch . . . with all the moving round the country. (*She stops*) I'm sorry, my name's Polya.

Verkoff And you're going to *stay* with this lot?

Polya Yes comrade, I have nowhere else to go. (*Looking down at the floor*) At the moment anyway.

Verkoff (*moving swiftly across the carriage to Nikolai*) Your pass and badge of office. Wear that at all times.

Nikolai (*as it is pinned on his fur coat*) My dear fellow, I assure you this is a major blunder, I urge you to reconsider while there's still time.

Verkoff (*turning at the door of the carriage*) I almost forgot the most important thing—what about food?

Sasha (*from the heart*) Food!

Verkoff (*with a mercurial smile at Sasha*) Yes, do you remember what it was like? (*To the adults*) Have you got enough, do you need some?

An agonized look from Sasha. Eugenia looks at Nikolai and then away. They wait for Nikolai. Silence

Nikolai No that will not be necessary.

Verkoff You're sure? You wouldn't be stupid enough to be too proud to ask—I'd have no patience with that. (*He watches their faces as he mentions each piece of food*) I can supply some eggs, meat, fresh cheese, smoked fish, fresh bread, (*he smiles*) that would mean soft doughy bread, baked today, like these rolls. (*He produces large rolls out of his deep pockets*)

Eugenia and Sasha turn away trying not to look at them

(*Holding out the bread*) Everybody looks away do they?

Sasha (*desperately*) Maybe we ...

Verkoff (*sharp, moving*) So you have managed to farm all your own food, unlike nearly everybody else in this area. I'm delighted to hear it. (*He leaves the bread lying conspicuously. Pointing at Eugenia*) You look magnificent madame. (*He stops in the doorway*) You are now working for me Nikolai Semenovitch—the Northern Railway and me. I don't know when we'll be seeing each other again but we certainly will be. (*With feeling*) I hope you're not going to let me down.

Verkoff exits

As soon as he's gone, Sasha bolts over and gets the bread he left behind. Eugenia also makes a move, less violent but almost as eager

Nikolai Don't disgrace yourself Sasha—charging after food like a starving dog.

Eugenia (*taking the bread*) Shall I? I'll divide it up.

Nikolai (*waving his portion away*) We do not need food from him. We are certainly not going to accept food like beggars.

The women and Sasha feast on the bread

I will provide all the food we need and more.

Sasha licks every crumb that is left

Polya Make it last ... not so quick Sasha, make it last as long as you can.

Eugenia (*smiling*) One's body can't cope with the shock at all. (*She leans against the wall*)

Nikolai (*calmly*) It appears we have been selected to spend time in these surroundings—something I didn't anticipate. So on my return we will divide it up. Eugenia ... this will be your room. (*He indicates an area in the middle of the carriage*) The child will be over there—(*pointing to the bunks*)—Polya's quarters will be down there—(*pointing to the area near the bunks*)—and the rest will be for my use, study, bedroom and morning room combined. (*He indicates the whole rest of the carriage*) We will keep to these. We may be able to arrange partitions when I return ...

The noise of a locomotive approaching is heard in the distance—calling down the line

Polya (*frantically*) His clothes and bed are not ready. I haven't had a chance to make it even passable for you, Barin. You will be away so long, and there hasn't nearly been time to unpack.

Both women are flitting about the carriage like terrified bats, as the sound of a locomotive coming is heard

(*Laying out his clothes*) The only pair of pyjamas that are left . . .

Nikolai There is no need to panic, they will wait for us.

Eugenia (*stopping, staring at him*) Nikolai, I think . . . please don't be angry with me . . . I think you will need me to come with you. Who will put out your clothes, with no manservant, and Liuba gone as well, nobody to do your laundry, find things for you to wear each day.

Polya It's not a job for you, madame.

Eugenia Let me come Nikolai, I won't be in the way, I won't touch anything. You know I won't bother you. You will never notice me, but you *need* someone . . . can I come? Please—(*suddenly loud*)—please let me come. I can make it all easier for you—(*loudly*)—let me . . .

Nikolai That will not be possible, my dear.

Polya You can't go on your own Barin, I must come . . .

Eugenia Make him see sense.

Nikolai Polya, you must stay with Madame. She must have the very best that is possible in the circumstances. (*To Eugenia*) Do nothing without Polya's help, my dear.

The locomotive is really loud and close, the sound of it braking and coming to a halt

I will take the boy—if he thinks he can manage the journey, I will take Sasha.

Sasha (*excited*) Me Papa? You want to take me?

The sound of the locomotive hissing to a halt

Eugenia Is that sensible, Nikolai? Neither of you are used to being on your own, he can't organize everything for you, Sasha can't deal with everything.

Sasha I can, I will.

Nikolai I am going to take the boy.

Eugenia (*urgently*) We must get more clothes for him, he'll need them for the cold.

Polya (*urgently*) It'll take at least two hours to get to the house and back, and I don't know how much is washed, how much is clean.

Eugenia (*moving*) Quickly, Polya, we'll have to go and get them. (*She looks back*)

Polya exits

Nikolai Don't worry, we will not leave before you come back.

Eugenia exits

Silence

(*Staring across at Sasha*) We will be alone together you and me.
Sasha Yes, Papa.
Nikolai Certain things have to be understood—the terms on which we
accompany each other. (*He pauses*) Sashenka, can you pass me that box,
yes that one there, give it to me.

Sasha gives Nikolai the mahogany box he came in with

I have something vital to occupy me—something of the highest import-
ance. If certain actions are taken—by me—it will be because of that. At
the moment nothing more can be discussed. (*He takes a pistol out of the
mahogany box; it gleams in the light*) Do you understand me?
Sasha Yes, but what are those other things in there, Papa?
Nikolai Diamonds, just a very few, all we were able to save from Moscow.
Sasha But, Papa ...
Nikolai There will be no problem, nobody will dare touch us.

Black-out

*The noise of the train immediately fills the black-out, moving through the
night, changing into the wail of the locomotive, then into screaming brakes, the
sound of their progress violently stuttering to a halt, then silence*

SCENE 2

*1,000 miles North of Moscow. The night carriage. The blinds are down. The
lights glowing. Sasha's arms are wrapped round himself. He is now wearing a
miniature version of his father's magnificent coat, and he is pulling it tightly
round him. Nikolai is sitting bolt upright and still*

Sasha Papa—we've stopped. (*Moving to the window*) I think we've arrived
somewhere again.
Nikolai We will not have heard of it whatever it's called.

Pause

Sasha (*by the window*) It's bloody cold anyway! God—(*trying to flex his
fingers*)—my hands, I can hardly move them. (*Moving from the window*)
I'm going to eat my rations for today, Papa.
Nikolai It is up to you when you eat.

Nikolai remains absolutely still. Silence

Sasha (*picking up a small brown morsel*) Except the taste of dried millet is
beginning to be ... rather revolting ...
Nikolai I have told you—use your imagination. What is it there for?
Transform the food.
Sasha Will you do it for me again?

Sasha begins to eat as Nikolai proceeds

Nikolai Imagine the delicate flesh, fish ... fresh-baked with a touch of sorrel the way Liuba used to cook it for us, pink, with a little butter and flaking——(*Suddenly stopping sharp*) How long is it since we left in this—how many days now?

Sasha I am not sure, we have stood still so often with just blackness out there, they don't even have stars here! I've got lost I think.

Nikolai (*calmly*) You promised me you were keeping count Sasha—what month is it, we must know that, is it still May?

Sasha I think it's May, or June, May . . .

Nikolai Put it up on the wall, say it is now Day twenty-one, notch it up on the wall. We start serious counting from now on, you must not lose count again, time has become important.

Sudden violent knocking on the door

Make yourself respectable.

Sasha pushes his hair straight, at the same time picking crumbs of food off his coat

Sasha Is there anything here people shouldn't find, Papa, that we should move before——

The door crashes open and two pale-faced guards in military uniform burst into the carriage with startling ferocity. Guard 1 is tall, thin, and in his late twenties, Guard 2 is burly, about ten years older, unshaven, hands stained with nicotine. Both guards are armed

Guard 1 Right! (*He stops for a second in surprise at seeing Nikolai resplendent in his coat, sitting in the magnificence of the carriage*) OK—could you stand up please. (*Sharply*) Come on stand up.

Guard 2 (*fast*) State your destination—arrival date, departure date, and nature of your business.

Guard 1 We need to see your travel permit and your identification card, where are they?

Guard 2 We're going to look at your luggage as well, so lay it out along here . . .

Nikolai My dear comrades, none of that need concern us.

Nicholai has remained seated, Sasha has stood

Guard 1 What do you mean that doesn't concern us—everything that comes down this line concerns us.

Guard 2 Where are you going for a start?

Nikolai (*simply*) I have no idea.

Guard 1 Do you know where you are now?

Nikolai I have even less idea of that—a remote settlement where it seems people have the sense not to live. (*He smiles*) I assume you didn't choose to be here. (*He looks straight at both of them*) Gentlemen, through some appalling error—for which I have yet to find the culprit—I am your new Telephone Examiner.

Silence

Guard 1 (*momentarily astonished*) You mean you ... you work for the Northern Railway?

Nikolai For the moment, yes. Why else do you think I would be here? (*He points to Sasha*) That over there is my son who is accompanying me on this mission. (*He smiles*) We are not going to waste our time in not believing each other, I would hardly invent such a story—there is no obvious advantage for me in having to wander up and down the line ... unless I officially *had* to.

A slight pause

Guard 1 No we believe you.

Guard 2 (*smiling*) If you say that's who you are—we believe you.

Guard 1 Forgive us comrade, we have been here so long, and we haven't seen anyone for several months, not since the men working on the line left.

Guard 2 (*with a sharp smile*) All we see is the occasional freight train, we wait by the line praying for lights to appear, howling for a train! And when one comes all we get are people staring down from the locomotive as they rumble past ...

Guard 1 But comrade we don't have much news here about telephones to give you—the poles haven't even arrived yet.

Nikolai (*calmly*) I expected as much.

Guard 2 Where are you from, comrade—which depot are you from?

Nikolai I'm afraid I have never been inside a depot. We are from Moscow, though we have been in the country for——

Guard 2 (*cutting him off*) Moscow! You're from Moscow. (*To Guard 1*) He's from *Moscow*, at last we've got someone ...

Both guards are exploding with excitement, questions tumbling out, cutting each other's sentences

Guard 1 (*loudly*) How are things there?

Guard 2 There's so much you'll have to tell us ...

Guard 1 What is happening? What is the latest news, are things easier, are more goods getting through to the shops?

Guard 2 Will we recognize the place? Are all the streets renamed? Is the new station built? They were just starting it, it was going to be enormous!

Guard 1 Is there still fighting in the East—are things quieter now?

Guard 2 (*with an earthy smile*) What sort of moving pictures are playing in Moscow—have you any of the latest jokes, we need a few!

Guard 1 We've had to sense what's been happening, imagine it all, from this distance.

Guard 2 We've missed so much already! We caught somebody's eye at the wrong moment.

Guard 1 We must have looked dumb enough!

Guard 2 Tell us what the good news is, start with that and——

Nikolai (*cutting them off; holding up his hand*) Gentlemen. Quiet. (*He pauses*) I have no news I'm afraid.

Guard 2 None? At all ...

Nikolai None. (*Facing them, calmly*) But we can do a transaction. We have little time to do it ... we have a drunken driver who decides to take off suddenly and with little warning ... so listen carefully because this is a matter of the utmost urgency. (*He pauses for this to sink in*) I need the following—which I am sure you will be able to provide. I need some foreign newspapers—any foreign newspaper. Any scrap of especially English or American journals you have, any stray piece that may have come into your possession off the trains from the northern ports.

Guard 2 (*taking it in*) Foreign newspapers ... foreign news.

Nikolai Second, I need some metal goods, any spare objects made out of metal of a transportable size, any metal appliances generally, everything you have.

Guard 2 Metal appliances?

Nikolai (*suddenly to Sasha*) Have I left anything out? (*Sharper*) Come on, have I?

Sasha Me Papa? ... *NO.*

Nikolai (*with a calm smile*) I am willing to pay for this of course, that goes without saying—I will pay one thousand roubles if what you supply is satisfactory.

Guard 1 (*bewildered*) One thousand roubles! As I understand it—all you want is some rubbish.

Guard 2 (*grinning*) We only have a limited amount of that round here—it's a very small station, take one step through the door and you've seen all there is to see.

Guard 1 We get a few odd things off passing trains, and there's some of the debris from the two large estates that were about fifty miles from here and were burnt by bandits, we've got a little of that.

Guard 2 It's all charred that stuff, you know it's burnt. (*He grins, eager to help*) You want some of that comrade? We can arrange it ...

Nikolai (*suddenly standing up*) I think I will have to examine it for myself— (*to Guard 2*)—show me the way.

Nikolai exits with Guard 2

Sasha (*loudly*) Papa!

Sasha is alone with the tall guard

Guard 1 (*looking at Sasha*) This is a magnificent carriage, comrade.
Sasha It needs cleaning.

The Guard moves round the carriage fascinated, looking at everything

You should have seen our apartment in Moscow, we had nine or ten rooms like this, with grand pianos in three of them ... my father has very high standards, he has the best of everything, usually ...

Guard 1 (*discovering with relish books in the carriage*) Books! Quite new!— I've had to read the same three books here over and over again. (*Flicking the pages of the official book, with an intrigued smile*) There is nothing in the ledger—none of the stops you have made have been recorded.

Sasha (*thinking quickly*) That was deliberate on my father's part—if we'd been captured by bandits there would have been no record.

Guard 1 (*looking at his father's clothes*) That is an extraordinary coat your father is wearing. (*With a friendly smile*) He's a very exotic visitor for us, something special. (*Turning to Sasha's coat*) All these clothes are foreign aren't they? (*Holding Sasha's coat*) The smell of women. I can detect that even after weeks; English clothes are they? (*He moves on, looking near the box with the gun in it*)

Sasha (*watching closely*) My father likes English things—even the pigs on our estate had English names, before they all died, Victoria, Hubert, Neville, and Lancelot, and Westminster.

Guard 1 (*picking up the box of guns*) What is this?

Sasha I think you may be exceeding your authority, my father said none of this must be touched. It's all *railway* business.

Sasha turns one of the lights low in the carriage

Guard 1 I just want a look, I won't do any harm.

Sasha (*really sharp*) Do you know who my father is—he's one of the most important men in Russia.

Guard 1 (*taken aback*) He is?

Sasha (*loudly*) Yes, you're not being visited by any old Telephone Examiner—by a run of the mill official just dropping in out of the night, he's one of the most significant people you're ever likely to meet.

Guard 1 Why?

Sasha Why? What do you mean why? (*Suddenly unable to answer*) Because ... he is a man of importance.

Nikolai enters, followed by Guard 2 wheeling a baby carriage, an ornate low baby carriage with faded roses painted on the side and full of charred remains from the great estate

Guard 2 smiles at Sasha who is staring in surprise

Guard 2 You won't be able to fit in this easily will you!

Nikolai (*indicating a corner*) Leave it there ... Sasha, pass me the money.

Sasha carries across the bag of money

Gentlemen, looking at this—(*he indicates the baby carriage*)—it is clear we will have to do better. (*Holding out money*) I am going to give you the one thousand roubles, some of which is for this, some of which is in advance for what you are still going to find for me—before we leave.

Guard 1 You want some more?

Nikolai And in return, if I have the opportunity—I will use my new office to put in a word for you. Gentlemen, I will recommend you be moved to a better and more important posting. Include your personal details in the next consignment you bring to me.

Guard 2 (*really loud*) We'll be back! (*Rushing to the door*) Don't you go till we're back. We'll certainly be back with more.

Both Guard 1 and 2 exit with urgency

Nikolai (*indicating the baby carriage immediately*) Are there any newspapers in there—have a look.

As Sasha searches through the charred remains ...

> We travel over a thousand miles—to find two young men going insane
> with loneliness! Feeling they're missing everything. The taller one is a
> pleasant boy, reminded me of one of the servants who left us for the war.
> The one with the rolling walk, what was his name? (*Suddenly back to
> Sasha*) Have you found some, Sasha? Bring me what you've got ...

Sasha moves over, handing him fragments of newspaper

> I've had no foreign news for so long—and this is the best they could do,
> like bringing water to a man dying of thirst but only a few drops at a time
> ... (*Staring at the tattered pieces of newspaper*) Where is this from?
> England, that's good ... that's very good.

Sasha also has a piece

> Look through your piece Sasha and tell me what you find.

Sasha What am I looking for, Papa?

Nikolai This does not look like a useful part of the paper. Dead diplomats
and garden parties. Find the date—it is vital we find the date (*without a
pause*) have you found it?

Sasha It's in English Papa!

Nikolai All that education he was given, how many governesses were
there—I lost count—and he can't even read the date in English.

Sasha (*struggling*) November twelfth, nineteen nineteen.

Nikolai My God! That's seven months ago. We will have to go through all
this, Sasha, column by column, inch by inch. (*Tossing newsscraps aside*)
This paper smells of cats. We will have to continue this by daylight.

Sasha I will try to make the tea for you ... I am getting better. I am still
practising. (*He goes about it as if preparing for a major operation*)

Nikolai I will tell you an interesting fact—I have never felt a kettle.

Sasha You haven't Papa?

Nikolai Certainly not when it has been boiling. I have never actually
handled one. (*He smiles*) I don't think I should start now.

Sasha (*looking out at the guns*) Do you think they really turn people off
trains like we were warned, making them walk into whatever's waiting for
us out there?

Nikolai It's more than possible. But why should anybody try to do that to
us? Don't worry ...

Sasha turns back to the tea. Suddenly Nikolai lets out a really loud cry

> What the hell do I do?

Sasha turns, startled

> How do I manage it now? ... Prevent it escaping ...

Sasha (*very worried*) What is it, Papa? Are you unwell?

Nikolai (*his voice has dropped to a rapid murmur*) Being incarcerated alive
... caged up like an animal ... it's not possible now ...

Sasha What is it? What's the matter? (*Suddenly moving closer*) What were
you looking for in the paper? Tell me, Papa.

Nikolai murmurs

What's happening? Tell me, please.

Silence

Nikolai (*his voice suddenly calm and authoritative again*) What have I always told you matters most, what is it our duty to do?
Sasha To . . . to achieve, Papa?
Nikolai Have you any idea what work I do?

A slight pause

Sasha No.
Nikolai When I went into that large office, what do you suppose I was thinking about?
Sasha Business?
Nikolai Business—don't show your ignorance child, you make me sound like merchants.

Nikolai is clutching the catch on the gun, Sasha watching tensely

Since there appears to be no-one here, other than ourselves, who could be listening . . . (*He looks straight at Sasha*) Nobody has ever been told what you are about to hear.
Sasha No, Papa.

Nikolai moves in the half-darkened carriage

Nikolai If you were to think your father had found a way of making the moving pictures talk—of recording sound on film and then so enlarging the volume so the picture talks. If you were to think I had found a way of doing this . . . (*After a slight pause*) Almost, nearly . . . you would be right.
Sasha (*very quietly*) You've done that! Nearly done that!
Nikolai Nearly, yes. In Moscow I found a way of printing sound directly on to film, but I can't unlock the answer to the final stage, how to enlarge the sound. The problem is frustratingly simple and the equipment required is reasonably rudimentary. If I can do that, I will be the first person in the world to do it.
Sasha (*hushed*) The first one . . . of all?
Nikolai Which will have a considerable effect on all our lives. Not merely fame and recognition on an international scale, but it will give me the power to acquire the resources and staff I need.
Sasha That was why you were looking in the papers.
Nikolai Yes, to see if on their theatre pages there is a comment on such and such a film performer's voice.
Sasha Do you think they could have done it already, before you?
Nikolai No. I am fairly certain I am three or four years ahead of the rest of the world. Naturally, I have no evidence for that, such a proposition is by its very nature unprovable. I sense I am ahead. But we mustn't dwell on that—if I think all the time about being overtaken we will go insane.

Silence

Sasha I have never been to the moving pictures.

Nikolai Neither have I.

Sasha (*surprised*) *You* haven't, Papa?

Nikolai No, never. Not in public. It is interesting, Sasha, don't you think, how time and time again the same idea happens in totally separate places at the same time—in completely different parts of the globe. They come out of the ether together. Simultaneous progress . . . But on this I have a real start.

Sasha Yes, Papa . . .

Nikolai (*suddenly really loud*) *But, my God, the odds, Sasha*—the odds against us are enormous. I am at least one thousand miles from Moscow, shut up in this wooden box—alone with a child. And on my return, the *women* have to live inside here, have to share this space with us . . . (*he pauses*) . . . a situation so bizarre I can hardly believe I have allowed it to happen to me.

Sasha I will help, I can do things.

Nikolai I didn't know being alone, could be so disturbing, left without our staff, servants, without any support.

Sasha (*very quiet*) It frightens me too, Papa.

Nikolai You must never admit to being frightened, Sasha. (*His tone lightening, picking up money*) At least there is one unexpected advantage—I have been given plenty of money.

Sasha For railway business . . . isn't it?

Nikolai (*suddenly looking at him sharply*) Have you taken in what I have just said, Sasha?

Sasha Of course, Papa.

Nikolai Look at me—look at me straight in the eye. You must learn to look people directly in the eye, anything else makes you seem dishonest.

Sasha Yes.

Pause

Nikolai Give me your word you will never repeat to anyone what you have heard tonight. The work must never be discussed in front of the women, or anyone, you understand.

Sasha I give you my word.

Nikolai You're old enough not to be terrified of ideas.

Sasha Yes, Papa.

Nikolai Good. It is stating the obvious Sasha—but this is a night of grave importance between us, more than any other.

Sasha I know, Papa.

Nikolai You must be careful to keep up your appearance Sashenka, especially when meeting ordinary soldiers like tonight . . .

Pause. They look at each other

You may go back to your room now.

Sasha (*moving across the width of the carriage*) It is a kind of race isn't it, Papa, what we're in?

Nikolai In a way.

Sasha And you'll come first?

Nikolai There can only be one result. (*Louder*) Let neither of us be in any doubt what is at stake from this moment on. It will need such energy, Sasha. (*Suddenly lifting the gun—pointing at the ceiling. Very loudly*) Come on you drunken bastard. Get this thing moving!

Sasha (*screaming*) Papa!

The door is thrown open, light pouring in. Nikolai makes no attempt to conceal the gun

Guard 1 moves into the doorway of the carriage and throws a large black bag of extra junk inside. It clanks as it hits the floor

Guard 1 (*with a friendly smile*) We found everything we could, comrade! Every scrap there is. Our names and personal histories are in there too, comrade, don't lose them! *We will meet again* (*he smiles*) when the new phone exchange is opened, we'll make the first calls! Goodbye, comrade, we won't forget you.

Nikolai Thank you my friend. I will not forget your promotion.

Guard 1 exits

(*As the door closes*) And comrade, tell our driver he is not to stop, don't let us stop at all now, till we hit the sea!

Black-out

SCENE 3

A hot sticky afternoon in the carriage, the two women, Eugenia and Polya, are alone. Several months later, 100 miles North of Moscow

Eugenia is dressed in a full-length white dress, long sleeves, lavishly dressed as if to entertain friends for an evening meal, but her clothes are now stained and streaked with dirt from months of being in the carriage. She is sweating profusely, constantly wiping her face. Polya, dressed in the black uniform but with bare legs, is kneeling on the carriage floor. Between deep intakes of breath she is half singing, half talking down a speaking tube, the sort that could have come from a large house, which snakes out of the carriage door, which is just open enough to let it through. Partitions are up around Nikolai's area. The table and chairs are now C. Polya continues to half sing, half gabble into the tube

Polya (*loudly*) Can you hear this ...? (*Then very quietly*) Is this loud enough? ... Seventy-seven, seventy-eight, seventy-nine, seventy-ten ... You see, after a day of this I can't even count anymore ... I am going to run out very soon ... my brain is throbbing, (*loudly*) can you hear it throbbing? (*Leaning her head forward*) Should be ear-splitting? Can you hear me at all!

Eugenia He will stop soon, I'm sure he must finish with you any moment, it's not physically possible to go on much longer.

Polya (*into the tube*) That's true of me, is it true of him? Maybe the master needs a drink ... (*Into the tube*) He is beginning to feel thirsty now ... getting a little cramped in that hut ... he's just thinking how welcome a cool, slow drink would be ... (*She continues to sing the song she began with very hoarsely*) I used to sing this while doing the stairs in Moscow, the master likes it, I don't think I ever want to hear it again after today. (*She continues breathing into the speaking apparatus a smattering of song, and a nursery rhyme; her neck is soaked in sweat*)

Eugenia If only he'd let me help you, he's always found the idea of me working extremely unpleasant. (*With a nervous smile*) He told me once he found the thought repulsive, (*lightly*) and I seem to be forbidden more than ever before to touch any of his work, even to glance at it. (*Looking at Polya kneeling on the floor*) Sometimes, Polya, I have an intense desire to go through everything of his.

Polya (*into the tube*) Can the master hear any of this ...?

Eugenia (*gently*) And now when he's divided up the carriage like the dacha, pinning us to this side. (*She smiles*) He's tried to shrink the house. (*She turns*) You know I've never slept in public before, till these past months, not with somebody in the room other than Nikolai.

Polya (*looking up*) Yes you squeezed yourself to the wall that first night didn't you, madame ... trying to hide in the luggage rack. (*Back to the tube*) Thirsty ... getting thirsty!

Eugenia Our neighbours, and my friends, would never believe this, that I ended up in this carriage ...

Polya (*finishing a verse of her song*) I wonder what I am doing all this for— (*a slight smile*)—after a time it does cross your mind, after fifty days, you do begin to get just a little curious. (*Into the tube*) What's the answer? Are you still there?

Eugenia At least you don't have to dress like I do—in this heat—(*holding herself*) —and, do you know what it feels like shut up in this?

Polya (*looking up*) I would go mad, madame, if I had to wear that all the time.

Eugenia There are good reasons for it. (*She moves*) As you know the master always wants me to have the best, the best of everything. He needs to live like that, regardless of where he is. I shouldn't be saying this to you, Polya but maybe because of us being Jewish, we were among the first Jewish families to be allowed to live in the capital. The master of course has never considered himself inferior to anyone ... so he always looked more part of Moscow society even than the oldest families, aristocratic in everything he chooses ... everything he does. So I *have* to wear all this, it's what he wants of me. (*Looking at Polya, she stops*) I really oughtn't to say such things to you.

Polya (*looking straight at her*) I know, Eugenia Michailovna ... it's all right. (*Loudly into the tube*) I am sure the master is no longer there— (*calling down*)—are you? He's walked off and left me singing to an empty railway line. (*Loudly*) So he won't notice, if I quite ... suddenly ... just ... (*very loudly*) stop. (*She gets up and moves away*)

Eugenia Is that wise, Polya?

Polya We'll see if there is any reaction. (*By the window*) I can't see him anywhere.

Eugenia (*with a self-mocking smile, indicating her stockings*) I wonder if I dare take these off? Do you think I should take the risk? If he notices you know how violently angry he can get. (*She hesitates*)

Polya Go on, he's too busy to notice.

Eugenia (*pulling off her shoes and stockings*) I suppose, Polya, that must seem foolish to you, a grown woman making such a business of taking her shoes and stockings off, making it seem an important event, but for me it is—(*she smiles*)—bare legs in the sun. (*She stretches her legs out*) My God that feels so good! (*She fans her dress*) Sweat trickling out, fresh air! Polya, why has it taken me this long? (*She moves to the window*)

Polya See, he *hasn't* come.

Silence

Eugenia (*by the window*) You realize we have no idea what is going on out there. None. We can only stand here, and wait for what is coming. I often think something is about to come out of the silence at us, suddenly appear down the line.

Polya Remember those corpses in the ditch by the dacha—all squashed up at one end with those hundreds of butterflies fluttering on top of them, murdered by bandits. I'll never forget those faces, their mouths open, one of the heads was sliced in half.

Eugenia I don't just mean the bandits and if they attack . . . (*She turns*) So many things may have changed *without us* knowing, Polya. (*She pauses*) Our street in Moscow will be completely different—it could have been torn down, they may be using it as barracks, soldiers sleeping in our bedrooms, or the apartment may have been swallowed up by Government offices (*slight smile*) the Transport Department, my old room full of bus routes, and filing cabinets in the bathroom . . . And the language will be changing, how you address people in the street. If I met somebody I used to know, have coffee with, this will sound stupid, but I start wondering what would I do, what would I call her? . . . What should I say?

Pause

We are so ignorant, Polya. (*She turns*) I am. It terrifies me sometimes. (*Suddenly breathing into the speaking tube*) Vastly ignorant. (*She looks up*) The master will never discuss his work with us and nor should we expect it.

Polya No?

Eugenia But, Polya, have you any idea why we have heard nothing from the authorities?

Pause

Polya Madame—I think there is something you ought to see. (*Moving towards Nikolai's private space*)

Eugenia (*hesitating*) What—we have to go in there?

Polya (*turning to face her*) I found these—I didn't know whether to show you.

Polya pushes her hand down the side of Nikolai's bed bringing out handfuls of large pristine white official letters with the Government seal on them

Eugenia They're not all official letters are they—and none of them opened? He must have opened some of them?

Polya Not one. (*She is producing letters from every crack and corner, from behind lamps, from under the bunks, from behind the stove*)

Eugenia The master never forgets anything—he didn't open these *deliberately*.

Polya (*scrambling on the top bunk, and near the roof*) There are plenty more, even under his sheets! These are the worst I think. (*She comes down with more*) Telegrams ...

Eugenia Because I'm not allowed to collect the mail Polya—I had no idea these had come.

Polya hands her the red-bounded envelopes

(*Staring down at them*) What do you think they all say—what do you think they want?

Polya We could open them, madame.

Eugenia Open his letters! If he found out ...

Silence

(*Suddenly pushing them into Polya's hand, with a nervous smile*) *You* open them. No, you can't read can you, Polya?

Polya Not quite.

Eugenia Give them back. I'm not that much of a coward! I'll do my own dirty work.

Polya crosses herself as Eugenia opens the telegrams

(*Reading the telegram*) "Urgent. Must have *news*, details Telephone Examiner immediately. What progress?"

Polya tears open another and gives it to Eugenia

"Why no news? Report state of work without delay. Most urgent. Reply essential." (*Looking at Polya*) I think we get the idea. (*Staring at the other envelopes*) I hope they don't get even worse.

Polya They better go back. (*She starts hastily pushing letters back into cracks*)

Eugenia God knows what else there is we don't know about.

Polya Well, madame—if you really want to see. (*Polya looks at her as she pushes the letters back*)

Eugenia (*quietly*) You better show me everything, Polya.

Polya There's this, the official ledger the master has to keep—(*indicating the huge bulky volume*)—there is not a word in it, it's completely bare.

Eugenia (*opening the huge ledger*) Not one entry? About the long trip he
  made with Sasha. (*Staring*) All these blank pages!
Polya And this is the most serious.
Eugenia What?
Polya (*indicating bags of money from the drawer*) He's spent some of the
  money, he's spent over half I think.
Eugenia And there is no record of it? (*She moves in agitation*) He must have
  spent it on all those things he brought back for his work—and the food he
  bribed off people to feed us with. I wondered how on earth he'd got it. I
  didn't dare ask. (*Sharper*) I didn't want to know.
Polya None of it is railway business—whichever way you look at it.
Eugenia (*facing her*) No, Polya. If he's misappropriated Government funds
  that could be disastrous—if it was discovered, even the master could be
  ... (*she stops*) ... even he ...

Pause

Polya The master could get shot, yes.
Eugenia (*sharper*) It's almost certain. (*She turns*) You mustn't mention any
  of this, Polya, that we've seen ...

*A noise at the door; they bolt across the carriage back to their places, as the
door opens*

Sasha enters

  (*Shouting*) It's you, Sasha—you shouldn't give us shocks like that, (*really
  loudly*) what do you think you're doing? Why didn't you knock? Don't
  you ever do that again!
Polya (*by the window looking out*) Where's the master? He's not right
  outside anymore ...
Sasha (*standing still*) I haven't seen him. I've been walking down the line by
  myself.
Eugenia Sasha—I have to ask you something serious, are you listening
  carefully?
Sasha (*watching closely from the wall*) What is it?
Eugenia Tell us what your father is doing.

Pause

  When you went off with him on that long journey for all those months—
  what did he tell you?

Pause

Sasha He didn't tell me anything.
Polya I don't think that's true—(*looking straight at him*)—you're lying,
  Sasha.
Eugenia We're here in the middle of the country and your father is doing all
  this work with Polya. Why?

Sasha is watching them

Polya Did he talk to you about his work? Yes or no?

Sasha (*quietly*) I think he did.

Eugenia Sasha—I realize we're not meant to know, normally I wouldn't ask. But you have to tell me, it could prove very dangerous to all of us if you keep it to yourself.

Sasha He told me everything he was doing.

Polya He did?

Sasha (*slowly*) But I was so scared while he was telling me, I was so frightened—I don't remember what he said . . . only that it's important. I can't even remember where we went.

Eugenia Sasha—is that true?

Polya I don't believe it.

Sasha Yes! I realized hours afterwards I couldn't remember what secret he told me.

Eugenia You can't even remember a part of it.

Sasha Nothing.

Eugenia (*suddenly moving*) One thing is certain, sooner or later somebody is going to follow these up, they are going to seek us out, to find what has happened. They'll burst in here one day, and that will probably be the end of all this.

Polya And us as well—probably.

Eugenia Yes. (*Looking at them*) And we can't escape anywhere, obviously—they will come after us. So . . . (*She moves, picks up a letter*) We've got to reply to these. (*Pause*) Write letters on his behalf and put something in here, Polya. (*She indicates the official ledger*) Somehow we've got to discover railway details, make up false records, fill up this with what he's discovered on his trip, so it appears he's made an effort.

Polya Give them something to read! (*She moves*) How are we going to do it?

Eugenia I don't know—have to try to remember the geography my governess taught me, my schooling, towns and small places in the northern district, all the bits that were always the most boring. (*She moves*) Maybe we'll find a map among his private papers we can use.

Polya I'll go through them.

Eugenia We have to lie, Polya—lies that won't be too specific, too obvious, about the things we found (*she corrects herself*) that the master found, "in such and such a place some progress was noticed, the workers conscientious"—maybe they will take so long to check with the northern depot, communications can't be good at the moment, that when they find out, it won't matter so much by then.

Polya Do you know anything about the Northern Railway, madame—I don't.

Eugenia No, or telephones. But we'll have to use our imagination—(*with a self-mocking smile*)—if I have any. We invent if necessary. (*Lifting a pen from the desk towards the virgin white pages, she writes*) "Day one, departed"—(*as she writes*)—the master must not know anything about this of course, he would tear it all out at once. We're just helping him because he's so very busy.

Polya Who are we more afraid of madame, him or them?

Eugenia (*sharper*) Polya—you shouldn't talk like that. (*Looking down*) What do you think the penalties are for doing this—they may be worse than for not doing anything at all.

Nikolai is standing in the doorway

Eugenia starts, closes the ledger, moves across the carriage holding it behind her

There you are—I was wondering where you were.

Nikolai is not even looking at her

Nikolai I thought you must have stopped, Polya. What happened to you?

He is staring down at Polya who's dripping with sweat, her hair matted back

Polya (*looking at him, then away*) I had to have a rest, Barin—so I am taking one . . .

Nikolai So it appears. (*He pauses*) Did we agree it was time to stop?

Polya (*quietly*) No, Barin.

Eugenia Nikolai, I want to ask you—have you had any messages from Moscow, any letters or telegrams from the authorities?

Nikolai From Moscow? Not of any significance. (*He turns back to Polya*) Polya, time is important to us, interruptions will prove very damaging. We are involved in a race against time.

Polya (*very quietly*) But I needed to have a break.

Nikolai Of course. I don't want you to be over-worked, Polya. If it has been a strain, then, certainly you must take a pause; we will start again in one and a half minutes.

Polya (*suddenly*) When I am ready Nikolai Semenovitch, we will go on, not before.

A startled pause

Eugenia (*worried by her boldness*) Polya . . .

Polya (*facing him*) I am so hot, I am filthy. Look at me.

Nikolai (*very firm, all his authority*) I need you to do it, Polya. (*Watching her defiant face*) You can have all my rations for the rest of the week, in return for more work tonight.

Polya I don't think you should try to bribe me, either. You must not interfere with the ration allocation, Barin—it will put the accounts in an even worse mess and we'll go back to starving. (*In silence she faces him*)

Nikolai She disobeys me—and she threatens me. (*Lightly*) And I cannot dismiss her—because there is no obvious replacement waiting outside. (*Sharper*) We will resume in less than a minute.

Polya Nikolai Semenovitch, when I go on—it will be because I want to and because Sasha says it's important, what you're doing, though he hasn't been able to tell us what it is.

Nikolai What I do *is* important, naturally. I wouldn't ask people to waste their time.

Polya (*nervously, but staring straight at him*) Are you going to tell me what it is, Barin?

Nikolai Your break for a rest is now over.

Polya I believe it *is* something important. But I would like to know what . . . what I am doing this for, Barin.

Nikolai (*ignoring this*) We must go on now. (*Sharply*) Polya, I have to have your help—I can't do without it.

Polya (*staring at him*) I know that. If I do it—it will be in my own time— (*with great dignity she kneels before the tube*)—which may be now, for a strictly *limited* time. (*Sharply*) You better go back to where you should be, Barin—or you'll be losing the time you've got me for. (*She begins to sing, on her knees, into the tube, a loud, piercing, powerful song*)

Black-out

Scene 4

The same. Several months later

Sasha is alone in the carriage. There is the distant sound of guns, the outside world encroaching. Grumbling gunfire, for the moment in the distance, sniping and occasionally the much larger sound of a field gun going off, shells falling— the noise is sporadic. Sasha is sitting at the far end of the carriage, holding one of the pistols and pointing it straight at the door. There is a sudden much louder sound of calls and shouts right outside the door, excited cries. Sasha stands holding the gun out in front of him pointing at the door

Sasha Who is that? (*Pulling back the catch on the gun*) Who is out there? I warn you! I am *armed*.

Eugenia and Polya burst through the door, their hair untidy. Distant gunfire behind them in the night

Eugenia What are you doing pointing that thing at us Sasha . . .?

Sasha I didn't know who was out there. (*With very real apprehension*) You never know what could come in from out there—especially on a night like this.

Eugenia and Polya are licking meat fat off their hands, having been cooking it outside, a new earthiness and directness in their manner to each other

Eugenia Do you think we burnt it? (*Glancing back through the door*) It looks like we may have burnt it!

Polya I'd completely forgotten the taste of meat—there're some things you could almost commit murder for, aren't there! (*Licking her fingers*) If only the comrade from Moscow had brought more of it.

Eugenia Took so long to pluck them—I had to restrain myself from just tearing the birds apart. (*She licks the last piece*) Little sputters of blood going everywhere—my cooking is so rudimentary, Polya.

Polya They won't notice.

Eugenia (*suddenly*) What are we doing? We're not ready! We have to prepare the table, they could be back any moment.

Sasha Papa's not going to make us all sit down to eat is he—he can't hold a dinner party during a battle.

Eugenia Of course—something small like that is certainly not going to stop him. If I could think of any possible way of preventing him I would do it, it's not exactly what we want the Commissar of Labour to see.

Polya and Eugenia run around the carriage producing a beautiful white table cloth from the drawers under the bunks, silver candlesticks and cutlery, fine quality china. During the following exchanges the table is prepared to its full splendour and the candles lit, gunfire in the distance beginning to roll towards them

(*Hearing the field gun*) Remember those nights in the apartment the first days of the Revolution, Polya, hearing the noise, just like this.

Polya The night everyone ran for shelter from the guns to the hotel across the street, during dinner.

Eugenia You were carrying all the luggage we could snatch in the time, weren't you. I piled you with so much silver you could hardly move. (*She imitates Polya's tottering figure*) You lurched down the stairs like this.

Polya Yes, silver was dropping behind me all the way down the street—if I tried to pick it up, I just dropped more . . .

Eugenia And the passage of the hotel filled with all those men keeping their hats on all night, walking up and down standing guard on us, everyone of them dressed like the master.

Polya Yes, but not quite as well.

Eugenia Hundreds and hundreds of them squashed into the corridor, I came out in the night and there was just this sea of bobbing black hats.

Polya (*laying the silver round the table*) And the cavalry officer, remember him, madame, what was he called? The one that sheltered in our room the next afternoon for a rest, I had to tie his tie for him when he woke, he'd never tied it for himself—he crawled out of the hotel during the shelling.

Eugenia And the master demanding where room service was.

The gunfire becomes a little louder

Sasha Is it nearer?

Eugenia God, I've forgotten half of it already—those extraordinary faces staring at me . . .

Polya (*moving round the carriage lighting all the candles*) Perfect strangers kept on giving me orders, pushing message into my hand, and saying, "Just run along the passage for me to such and such a room."

Eugenia If I'd known what it meant—I would have remembered it more. I knew things wouldn't be the same again, but I just had a sense of total irritation all the time constantly being kept awake, the firing, like somebody kicking you in the ankles all the time, so you're in a terrible nervy temper—feelings hardly matching the size of the occasion and how near we were, (*sharply*) how inadequate one's immediate responses often are, mine anyway. (*She moves; loudly*) Was that them? Are we ready?

Polya Sasha put that gun away . . . No, hide it properly, not there, that's the most obvious place.

Sasha had put it under his pillow, he puts it behind the stove

Eugenia Polya, we have to do everything in our power, and I mean everything to make sure the Commissar of Labour doesn't interrogate the master, steer him away from anything about railway business, and we can't let him mention his work.

Polya Yes. (*Kicking the tube into a corner*) If he sees anything we say it's part of the heating system.

Pause

Eugenia You know if we got this food in here now, and we were able to move this carriage on our own, we could ride off with all this for ourselves, slide off down the line away from danger ...

Verkoff enters with Nikolai. Verkoff is flushed from watching the gun battle

Nikolai They are waiting to feed us.

Verkoff We should be safe in here. (*To Eugenia*) I hope I'm right, you look concerned. What a night! We got quite close to the action didn't we, Nikolai Semenovitch, caught glimpses of them through the trees!

Nikolai (*calmly*) I saw nothing, the smoke got in my eyes.

Sasha Who are they fighting?

Verkoff They are flushing out some white bandits. Some renegade soldiers and a collection of bandits have teamed up, a really seedy bunch! But they've got themselves three old guns somehow and are roaming the forest—(*he smiles at the gunfire*)—shouldn't be many of them left by morning.

Nikolai (*staring down at the table*) There are no table napkins, Polya—for some reason they have been forgotten.

Polya rushes for them as Nikolai pours wine

This is the best bottle I have left, it's maybe a little thin.

Verkoff (*looking around*) What have you done to this place? Railway life seems to be suiting you, comrade!

Nikolai Despite the monstrous administrative error—a little progress has been possible.

Verkoff What monstrous error is that?

Eugenia Polya! You better bring the food at once—(*sharply*)—as quickly as you can.

Polya exits with a silver tray

Nikolai (*with a charming smile*) What you have singularly failed to rectify. Do not be fooled by the appearance of luxury—you have left us in a corner where even the peasants do not live ... when it rains you can hear the rats squeaking and scuffling underneath, some of them poke their heads through to peer at me. (*With a slight smile*) And they are free and I am caged.

The sound of guns, all the time slightly nearer

Verkoff Don't worry—they won't be able to shoot straight. (*Looking at Nikolai's table*) If they could see what was going on inside a Government train!

Polya comes in with the food—small roasted pieces of some bird, scattered across a large silver platter; the amount of meat is tiny, on the huge tray

Eugenia (*nervously*) Here's the food, comrade.
Verkoff And we're going to be eating it off English silver?
Nikolai Of course it's English.
Verkoff Only the best naturally!
Nikolai (*with a charming smile*) I have never been rich enough to afford to buy anything but the best.

Polya is dividing the meat up, the smell of freshly roasted game filling the stage

(*Unabashed*) In England you find quality everywhere. An immensely civilized, comfortable place—arriving there is like sliding into a warm bath—(*he stares at Verkoff*)—which nobody is suddenly going to try to empty. People never argue there, the clothes are beautifully made, the service superb.

The food is now ready in front of them

Verkoff (*staring at him, suddenly very loud*) Nikolai Semenovitch you are the biggest snob I have *ever* met and I have met a few. (*Pointing at him*) It's shameless! And it gets *worse* with him!
Eugenia (*hastily*) My husband finds it difficult to break old habits.
Verkoff The way you dress! Even here where nobody at all can see you—a Jew that behaves like an archduke, who had to be the best-dressed man in Moscow. Someone that can serve a meal like this on his family silver in the middle of a forest, during a battle!
Nikolai If the mind is to function it has to be looked after, if as simple——
Verkoff (*with a sharp smile*) You know you could antagonize certain people behaving like this, it has been known! (*Looking straight at him*) It's as well you've been employed on railway business isn't it. (*Really loud, pointing at Nikolai's feet*) I shouldn't think there's another pair of shoes left like that in the whole of Russia!
Nikolai Comrade—I thought you had a revolution so you would be able to dress like me—not I like you.

They look at Verkoff. Silence, followed by a sudden loud laugh

Verkoff Did you hear him? (*After a pause*) People have been shot for saying less.

The sound of shelling, growing gradually closer all the time

Nikolai I don't necessarily disapprove of everything that has happened—(*indicating himself*)—though of course a mistake like this should have been avoided. Despite that—the astronomical incompetence that was allowed before, that was freely tolerated, it amazes me now.

Verkoff (*sharply*) He admits that much.

Nikolai (*incisively*) Before it happened there was an unhelpful nervousness too—a general unease, people hurrying faster between the front door and their carriage, myself included.

Verkoff He had to run into his house!

Nikolai Yes, a listlessness when in public places, (*a slight smile*) . . . Waiters became unpredictable. (*He pauses*) There was a constant sensation of something pressing, pressing down on one like a weight on the walls—needless to say I was completely unaware of it until everything "erupted" . . . then quite suddenly I realized it had been there all the time.

Sasha (*suddenly really loud, famished*) Papa—*please* can we start, aren't we going to eat now! We've been *waiting* to eat this—I can't wait any more, please let us begin.

Silence

Nikolai Sasha. (*His manner is truly formidable, dangerous*) What is the meaning of this? Have you forgotten there are guests present?

Pause

Remove yourself to your room and eat there . . . and take a knife and fork, I will not have you not eating properly, you are not to eat with your bare hands. (*He turns back to the table*) Let us begin.

Everybody falls on their food violently except for Nikolai

There is no hurry, the food will not run away.

The gunfire is getting nearer

Verkoff We want to eat before we die! (*Tearing at meat furiously*) my family were all butchers you know . . .

Eugenia looks nervous

But they all hated meat. (*He looks up at the finished eating*) If I'd known you were hungry I would have brought some more . . .

Eugenia is trying to resist eating with her fingers. Polya is sitting separate, pulling meat up to her mouth, a sound comes out of her, a crying noise, curling her body to the wall

Eugenia What is it Polya—are you all right?

Polya Oh yes—it's just slightly good. (*She makes the deep famished cry again*) Just a little nice you know.

The gunfire is now very close, Verkoff looking at Nikolai presiding over the table

Verkoff (*with relish*) Look at him now! I would love to see the shock people have as you go about your railway business—that I would pay to see. (*Loudly*) I would queue to see it!

Eugenia (*nervously*) Have some more wine comrade, here . . .

Verkoff (*loudly, moving round, his fingers stabbing out*) They have started sending out special trains from Moscow with performing groups on them, young people, actors, musicians, doing sketches, spreading across the country, explaining, informing, communicating—the idea of *them* passing *you* at some remote station, it is wonderful. Rolling back the door of the carriage and finding this apparition—this figure looking as if he's stepped out of the last century, if not before, dressed for going to the opera, waving his stick at them and shouting, "Go away, don't interrupt me, I am too busy, my work is vital!"

Nikolai Why should it be extraordinary?

Verkoff I love the idea! (*A sharp look*) What rich times these are, eh, Nikolai Semenovitch!

Nikolai (*calmly*) It is only children and Government Officials that can't hold two totally separate—seemingly opposing—ideas in their head at the same time.

A shell breaks closer to the carriage as the battle rolls towards them. Eugenia and Sasha instinctively duck

(*Calmly*) I am engaged in a struggle where the outcome can never be totally guaranteed—but it is a reasonable prediction to make that this carriage will become as famous as the one they signed the German surrender in, and we are by coincidence also in a forest.

The noise of sniper fire is suddenly closer as well

(*Glancing at Verkoff*) If I do what I am capable of—this, my appointment, will be the highlight of your career.

Verkoff (*with a broad smile*) As Telephone Examiner!

Nikolai (*lightly*) You will be erecting plaques on this wall in years to come and showing your grandchildren. People will be coming here to inspect where it was all done—(*a charming smile*)—though for the convenience of the public they may wish to move the carriage nearer to civilization.

The loud whistle of a shell seemingly descending directly above them hanging in the air for a second, as the battle reaches them

Verkoff Careful! They're getting really close. Take cover!

Polya, Sasha, Eugenia move over to the bunks, Verkoff crouches, only Nikolai remaining sitting absolutely erect as the shell explodes directly behind the carriage, a bright white flash behind the windows, the walls of the carriage shaking violently; the wine falls over spreading a huge red stain over the table cloth and dripping down the side. Nikolai is still sitting absolutely erect

Nikolai (*calmly, seriously*) I can assure you my friend—the modern world is grinding around in this carriage, forcing its way out, coming into existence right here, but any disturbance now does not help.

The loud whine of a second shell descending

I'd appreciate then being reduced to a minimum.

The second shell explodes behind the carriage

Having to operate surrounded by one's family . . . women and children, is
a problem.

*Silence. A pause in the bombardment, Polya and Eugenia look up from the
bunk*

Verkoff (*up again, moving sharply round the carriage*) It has stopped for the
moment. I must get my inspection over before it starts again.
Eugenia What inspection is that, comrade—I thought you'd seen every-
thing you'd come to see.
Verkoff The official records of course. Where has our money been going?
Eugenia (*sharply*) Money?
Verkoff (*to Nikolai*) Until recently we were not getting any replies from you
to any of our messages.
Nikolai I was not aware I had replied at all.
Verkoff (*rifling through the papers on the desk*) How were they all? I haven't
seen them for months. How is Varyov, the one with half a moustache, and
the little squat ugly one, who always has his flies open, what's his name?
At the depot? How have you been getting on with him?
Nikolai I will not conceal facts, I cannot lie to you, I have never been to the
depot.
Polya (*moving across the carriage with the huge volume*) Here is the ledger—
all the records we have comrade are *here*.
Nikolai I can save you wasting your time.
Eugenia Nikolai, you must move from there, the wine's dripping, why don't
you come here?

Polya crosses herself as Verkoff flicks the pages of the ledger

Verkoff (*flicking, reading*) "Progress considerable" . . . "work satisfactory"
. . . "tolerable progress" . . . This is such an extensive record, (*he strides*)
places I have forgotten existed, places I've never heard of—you have been
conscientious, comrade! I must keep this.
Eugenia (*sharply*) Keep it? Why comrade?
Verkoff (*with a sharp smile*) To study, to read at nights. (*Slamming the
ledger shut*)
Nikolai You must show me, you must let me see this, there's been a mistake,
I wouldn't wish you to leave here with a false impression.

The gunfire is further off again now, to the side of the carriage

Verkoff I must go—I must leave while I can still get out.
Eugenia Yes, comrade.
Verkoff (*sudden really loud, with a volatile smile, full of relish*) You're an
impossible man, Nikolai Semenovitch—what an absurd creation we have
here. What an infuriating bastard. (*He moves around the carriage*) And he
flaunts it!

*Verkoff suddenly physically lifts Nikolai up off the ground in a single
movement and holds him like an enormous doll*

He revels in it. (*Holding him*) He's got made at the Ritz stamped on his
arse. He has! I can feel the crest right here.

Nikolai (*calmly with great authority*) Put me down, comrade.

Verkoff (*carrying straight on*) Hang you up on this peg as an exhibit in your own carriage—an item for future generations to wonder at. (*He puts him down and points*) This is the man I made Telephone Examiner, see! I did! (*Moving—very loud*) I will tell you this my friend, I will never forget you—I will *not* forget you.

Nikolai Somebody else said that to me recently.

Verkoff Has that penetrated that thin skull—gone all the way down. (*Suddenly his tone changes, as he produces an envelope from his pocket; seriously*) You have new orders now. Their contents will not surprise you I think. Read them and goodbye.

Nikolai (*seeing Verkoff at the door*) I must accompany you then.

Verkoff (*to Eugenia*) He wants to escort me off his "estate"!

Gunfire in the distance

Come on then before it's too late.

Verkoff exits

Eugenia (*loudly*) Kolia!

Nikolai turns in the doorway

You will be careful, don't say anymore—just let him go. Leave him.

Silence

Nikolai Am I to understand you are giving me instructions . . .

Eugenia No, I'm just warning you. I mean . . . (*looking down*) . . .

Nikolai There are obviously things going on here—things you have done, Eugenia, that I do not know about.

Pause. He looks at her

We will discuss them when I return.

He exits

Polya (*turning, staring across at Eugenia*) Eugenia Michailovna. (*After a slight pause*) We did it!

Eugenia I don't know . . . I couldn't tell . . .

Polya (*very excited*) We did, we did! (*She physically catches hold of Eugenia, squeezing her arm*) We've *survived* the visit, haven't we . . . we made it work, we've managed it.

Eugenia Yes . . .

Polya God, every time he looked round, though, the Comrade Commissar, my heart started going like this—I'd rather have been out there when the guns are going off. (*She looks at Eugenia*) We did all right, didn't we?

Eugenia I hope so . . . (*Suddenly urgent*) Polya, you'd better go after the master, I think; we can't take the chance, keep by his side, don't let him explain anything.

Polya I'll catch them. (*Running across the carriage to grab her shawl*) I'll talk non-stop, gabble all the way to the comrade's car. Nobody else will get a word in . . .

Polya exits

Eugenia and Sahsa are alone—the huge red wine stain dripping off the tablecloth, the charred chewed bones of the bird spread across the tablecloth

Eugenia (*urgently*) Have we managed it, Sasha?

Sasha Mama?

Eugenia (*moving across the carriage*) The orders? (*Sharply*) Where are the new orders? (*She tears open the envelope*) We've being moved at once to Moscow. (*She stares at the paper*) In this carriage. They're sending a locomotive to take us across country at night, next week.

Sasha What does that mean? Is it bad news? (*Watching her*) What are they going to do with us?

Eugenia That's all it says. (*Very quietly*) We are going to be met at Moscow. (*She moves across the carriage*)

Sasha (*worried*) By whom, Mama?

Eugenia (*moving, thinking*) We could have all died on several occasions over these past months because of your father—left to his own devices that might have happened ... Have we helped him or not? *Did I do the right thing?* (*Surprised at herself*) Without even asking him! I wish I knew more. Will he ever let me help him again if I have the chance?

Sasha What do you think will happen in Moscow?

Eugenia There is no telling. (*Louder*) We mustn't lose the protection of being here, Sasha—we must fight to keep it, the protection of his job, I am *not* going back to starving, chewing nuts crawling on one's knees licking the ground.

The sound of gunfire suddenly louder again

If we lose this, if we're thrown off here, we don't all survive. It's as simple as that. (*She turns; sharper*) What are all those things he talked about ... grinding around in this carriage ... modern ... going to be the highlight of people's lives. What did he mean?

Sasha I don't know, Mama.

Eugenia (*suddenly*) I am going to find out what he's doing. Private space or no private space—I have to know. (*She pulls the partition down around his part of the carriage*) Why haven't I done this before. (*Pulling out his drawers*) What am I hunting for? Will he have written it down. Will it suddenly be here, staring at me? (*She pulls open the cases*) Tell me—do you feel different, Sasha?

Sasha What do you mean, Mama?

Eugenia What do you think different means? (*She is emptying Nikolai's drawers and pulling open all his hidden places, her mood excited. As she goes through his papers; lightly*) You know Sasha, my whole adult life, every waking moment seems to have belonged to your papa ... his world, his determination, the power of his moods ...

Another piece of furniture is upturned

So where is it? What *is* his work Sasha, where's the answer?

Sasha (*watching her from a distance*) I *told* you, I don't know, Mama.

Eugenia (*excited as a flare goes up outside the window*) Oh if only he'd let me do something your Father—let me do more. (*She is framed in the light of the flare, sensual energy*) What is happening to us, Sasha? What is happening to me? (*She turns powerfully towards Sasha*) You don't like me talking like this ... do you?

Sasha No, Mama, it's all right. (*He is watching her closely*)

Eugenia It's because you have never heard it before. Not used to it. (*She moves towards him*) You look older, Sasha ... (*Touching his face*) Is that hair, a beard, there's a man growing here. (*She returns to Nikolai's belongings that she has strewn across the stage. She pulls out of the last pigskin case a bulky film camera, smothered in dust*) Just an old camera! That can't be it. He hasn't used it since we arrived in here. It's covered in dust. (*She blows dust off the camera*)

Sasha (*staring down at the camera, pushing it with his foot*) Is it possible do you think for somebody to have new ideas, somebody who never goes out, never talks about it to anyone (*watching her*) is that possible? Somebody who can't boil a kettle?

Eugenia Who can't boil a kettle?

Sasha Nobody ... no-one.

The noise of a shell whistling and screaming down towards them exploding behind the carriage

That was very close. They're coming back!

Eugenia snuffs out some of the candles and pulls Sasha towards her, in the middle of the carriage

Eugenia (*her mood strangely excited*) You should remember tonight Sasha—write it down, we've constantly been on the edge of great events, do you realize, just outside, in Moscow and here on the edge of a battle, so near we've been able to smell them. (*Facing him*) You will remember it for me? You will?

Sasha Yes, Mama.

Eugenia Better than you have been? We both will.

Sasha (*staring at her as the shells begin to fall*) I had a dream about Papa earlier today—they tore off his clothes and tied him to a gate in a field and shot him in the head. Do you think we're going to be all right—or are they going to try to kill us. (*He stares at her*)

Pause

Eugenia Do your dreams often come true?

Sasha (*after a pause*) Yes.

Eugenia Let it not be for a while then. (*A slight smile*) Not quite yet. (*Touching him*) You never know we may be lucky.

The Lights fade to Black-out

ACT II

The carriage. Moscow Railway Shunting Yards. 1924

Cold, snow outside, the sound of the rail shunting yards. A military band can be heard rehearsing in the distance, stopping and starting, sudden, dissonant, edgy noise, silence, then rapid brassy playing, sometimes ceremonial, sometimes mournful, little spiky bursts. Sporadically heard through the scene, as the musicians rehearse. We do not hear the main tune of the piece they are playing in its entirety

The carriage is full of steam, clothes hanging up to dry, towels, sheets and other clothes including underwear drying on the bunks, and hanging from the ceiling. Much more informal look to the grandness of the carriage, piles of apples, carrots, and potatoes, and other food stored, kitchen utensils hanging up

Polya is pouring hot water from a large white china jug. Eugenia, dressed only in her petticoat, kneeling by an enamel bath having her neck washed, steam pouring from the jug as hot water slops into the bath. Sasha, dressed in plain clothes and looking older, is pacing the carriage learning something from a book

Eugenia (*in mock terror*) Stop it Polya, stop! It's too hot, you're going to boil me alive ... don't. (*She screams as you do when you're being scalded*) Don't! See, I'm going scarlet.

Polya (*standing over the bath*) Don't you dare move till I've finished.

Eugenia (*as water falls on to her arms, shrieking in half-mock pain*) Polya, it hurts, you've never known such pain! For goodness sake stop ...

Polya (*smiling*) You're not going to move till I tell you to.

Eugenia I'm going to be late you realize, terribly late, and I can't be today. (*Getting up, laughing*) You're going to let me go. (*She gets up*)

Polya What's so special about today?

During the following exchanges, Eugenia dresses at a furious rate, pulling on heavy socks and shoes, plain black skirt, and brown sweater and at the end a long great coat— she is totally transformed. As she shivers furiously, her bare shoulders shaking

Sasha (*pacing up and down the carriage, trying desperately to memorize facts*) The Moscow drainage system is now the envy of the world ... the weight of refuse now being dealt with has increased at six times in as many years—(*he looks at his notes*)—no four times, . . . cutting through the old foundations of the city . . .

Jarring notes of the music outside

Polya (*shouting out of the window*) Play in tune can't you! (*Turning*) If we have to have a band just out there—why can't they play something a bit better. (*Looking at Eugenia*) Why are you rushing so much?

Eugenia We start making the new timetables today—and we have to notify all the regions of the new ticket price, it's going to be a rush to make the deadline.

Polya (*a sharp smile*) Sounds as if it can wait five minutes to me.

Eugenia It's an office full of men. I'm the *only* woman there still—so I have to be on time. (*She smiles as she dresses*) The whole of that building smells of men.

Polya Bring some of them back here sometime!

Eugenia (*fast, smiling*) I'm getting a little less afraid of them. They keep on wanting to know where I come from, really curious about us having the tiny apartment but also being allowed to keep this. (*She indicates the carriage*) They want all my personal history. I give them a little bit at a time.

Polya At the mail sorting office we've got a miserable collection of males at the moment. People just "passing" through . . . (*she smiles*) . . . means a lot of wandering hands! (*Suddenly she shrieks with laughter*) But *nobody* discovered about my reading, you were right, how basic it was, (*loudly*) deeply basic at the start. Me peering at letters, hopefully throwing them in the right holes, letters going off in all directions. If people had bad handwriting they didn't stand a chance with me!

Eugenia (*with a teasing smile*) To think some letters travelling *two thousand* miles and then having to end up with you, Polya!

Polya Now I'm really efficient—there isn't enough post to keep me quiet— (*To a sombre noise out of window*)—shut up!

Sasha (*testing himself*) At the deepest point in the drainage system—how deep is it?

Polya Sasha, what on earth are you doing?

Sasha It's another school dissertation, you could either write about a member of your family—or an aspect of Moscow.

Eugenia (*incredulous*) And you chose the drains.

Sasha I deliberately picked an unpopular subject so I was bound to do well—I mean nobody knows anything about the city drainage system and what's found in it, I'm certain none of the teachers do.

Eugenia (*with a slight smile*) And what about your family, does nobody know about them?

Sasha (*hesitating for a split second*) No . . .

Eugenia (*moving very fast, putting her scarf on*) I'll probably kill myself, won't I, going from being that hot into that cold, it's really snowing, but I *will* not be late. Where's my identity card, (*moving*) I haven't seen Nikolai for days, it seems . . . (*By the door, as she pulls it open*) Come on! Head down and charge.

She exits into the cold

Polya (*calling after her, as she pushes the door shut*) Don't run in the snow
you'll fall on your arse. (*Loudly, smiling*) You will anyway.

As Polya closes the door, the band plays a burst

What an unearthly noise! Why do you think they're rehearsing that sort
of music?

Sasha (*by the window, jumping up*) I can't see them. Just out of sight, as
usual! There've been a lot of comings and goings ... soldiers arriving by
train last night, cars moving across the shunting yard.

Polya is looking across the width of the carriage at him

Polya Yes, I heard officials from all over the country had been arriving
since early this morning. I think something has happened. Now—for you,
Sasha. Do you need a wash? Very definitely I should think.

Sasha Do I? (*His manner is strangely adult*)

Polya Ages since I washed you. (*Something stops her*) I don't think I even
ought to try now.

Sasha (*pulling his top off, washing himself*) No—I don't think so.

Polya (*with a sharp smile*) You used to call for me with that noise, used to
bray for me remember, Pol-ya, that's how it went.

Sasha (*lightly*) You were always slow in answering too.

Polya (*doing the call*) "Pol-yaa make my bed" ... "wash me" or in the
middle of the night "I'm afraid, come to me quick, I'm frightened of the
demon with three heads".

Sasha What demons? I was stupidly over-sensitive. (*Looking at her, with a
slight smile*) When you came to me, bent over the bed, you had that
particular smell—I've always been meaning to tell you.

Polya (*loud*) What smell?

Sasha The cheese smell of course—all those days you did it, and it stayed
with you.

Polya (*loud*) Did what?

Sasha (*teasingly*) When you carried cheese—before we found you and
brought you to Moscow. You coming to the house from the village
wearing that long black dress, so long it scraped the ground carrying
those horrible curd cheeses, that smell was always there.

Polya (*angry, loud*) You're not trying to tell me Sasha it's still there!

Sasha Maybe.

Polya (*moving towards him*) You rude little bastard. Come here.

Sasha You haven't got a hope of catching me anymore.

They circle each other

Polya You know what *you* looked like then, in your little velvet suit and
floppy golden curls,—a puppet child.

Sasha I know I looked hideous! (*A sharp smile straight at her*) A very good
example of what used to go on. (*He moves past her, dodging her, getting to
other end of carriage*) You know Polya, I still can't dress the way I
want to.

Polya (*mocking*) That's very serious.

Sasha It is! I manage to hide the expensive gloves and scarf he makes me wear—(*moving*)—and when he's not looking I wear this coat—(*he indicates his grey coat*)—and then I look exactly the same as everybody else, almost *normal*. (*Very loud*) Except for these shoes, Polya—these terrible English shoes!

Polya What's the matter with them?

Sasha What do you think, it's like they're on fire, they stand out a mile, everyone points at them. (*He starts kicking the walls, smashing his feet against the corners, rubbing furiously*) I try to beat them down, I scuff them all the time, on the way to school every day.

Polya (*laughing*) But they won't change!

Sasha They're indestructable, they're so bloody strong, nothing I do makes any difference.

Sasha sits, his legs splayed out, mauling the shoes, Polya laughs

When I have to go for a walk with Father—I keep well behind him.

Suddenly he's imitating his father in the middle of the carriage. Polya begins to laugh

He looks so ridiculous, strolling along, in that great coat, with a cane, in the shunting yards, he among all this rolling stock here, freight—being unloaded, and there he is saying good-morning to everyone with a wave, like he's greeting farm labourers on his estate.

Polya (*watching him*) What does it matter? If he thinks like that, I expect they enjoy it.

Pause

Sasha (*with a slight smile; suddenly*) I tell people at school, I tell everyone he's an engine driver.

Polya (*surprised*) You don't do that Sasha! You wouldn't.

Sasha I do. (*Suddenly serious; calmly*) Do you realize, Polya, he has never done a proper day's work in his life, not one, he's never even contemplated it!

Polya Of course he works—he has *his* work.

Sasha What work? You don't mean this I take it?

Polya (*defiant*) Yes.

Sasha The idea we have believed this for so long, haven't admitted what's happening, it's extraordinary—not even questioning it, just whispering about it when at last he's left that corner and gone out.

Polya *I* have never whispered about it.

Sasha If I think of all the days since I was small of creeping round the place in case I disturbed him ... (*Loudly*) The truth is and we've got to face it, Polya—(*pointing at Nikolai's corner*)—this is all useless, utterly useless— he's just a self-deluding old man.

Polya (*shocked*) Sasha ... (*Then sharply*) He's not that old for a start!

Sasha (*incisively*) He contributes nothing, he receives money from the State for another purpose entirely, he has official duties which he ignores completely—(*loud*)—absolutely totally ... that's the part I can't forgive, he takes the money which isn't his and then plays with his little pieces in a corner——

Polya Just plays, does he!

Sasha He can't even fit these scraps together.

Polya (*watching Sasha's sharp, piercing stare*) I had no idea you were growing into such a nasty young——

Sasha No, no, listen. (*Very incisive, trying to persuade her*) Examine the facts, Polya, please, for the first time in your life, this is very important. (*Moving with a commanding tone*) It is not just that we have never seen him consult a single technical journal, or even use a single technical term when he's talking——

Polya (*sharply*) So?

Sasha We are being asked to believe that someone obsessed by eating off the right silver plate, using the right silver fish fork, is doing something of significance, is involved in technological progress!

Polya (*defiant*) Yes!

Sasha (*continuing straight on*) It is a ludicrous proposition, obviously preposterous—it doesn't stand up to a moment's analysis. I mean he can't even boil a kettle—(*loud*)—he can't even boil a bloody kettle, Polya.

Polya Nor could you till recently. (*She is watching him*)

Sasha He told me what he was doing.

Polya He did?

Sasha At the time you asked me I still remembered—but now I've long forgotten. He is a dilettante, Polya, a perfect instance of somebody refusing to change, placing his own needs above everybody else's—his individualism destroys others. I am *asham*ed, Polya, to be seen with him, to be associated with him in anyway.

Polya (*moving across*) You've got to stop this, Sasha—you will stop it or I'll make you.

Sasha Deny it if you can ... you know you can't.

Polya Look at you—(*catching hold of him, catching hold of his legs*)—burrowing away to try to be as ordinary as possible ...

Sasha (*incisive*) And what's more you still can't tear yourself away can you—you can't bring yourself to leave despite having a room of your own now ... (*loud*) ... you still come back for more—and he goes on exploiting you just the same.

Polya (*loud, close*) Don't you start patronizing me—give me lectures about what I should be doing, (*very loud*) it's *my* affair, don't you dare tell me what to do—if you ever talk to me like that again ...

Polya seizes the fur coat Sasha does not wear any more. The band is still playing outside

Sasha I am just explaining the situation to you, Polya.

Polya (*pinning him to the wall*) What a crude little animal you're turning out to be—afraid to stand out in a crowd are we? (*She starts forcing him into the fur coat*) We'll see to that!

Sasha is trying to resist; they grapple by the window. Polya, winning, gets the coat half on, forcing his arms above his head as she has him pinned against the wall

Nikolai enters. He stands poised in the doorway in his fur coat, fur hat, and stick. He removes his hat and gloves staring past them into the carriage

Nikolai Is the place ready for me again? The washing is still out. (*He moves into the carriage*) Bring me my tea, Polya, my tea and notes, my gloves need to dry …

Nikolai hands Polya his wet gloves, putting his stick on the table, and sits in the chair that is always reserved for him. Sasha leans against the wall watching Polya run around, folding up the washing

I have news, I have sent off through the emergency railway messenger service for a special delivery for my work—it is an unexpected bonus of this job, which is proving more and more useful.

Sasha and Polya exchange looks. Nikolai smiles

(*Turning*) Where is the tea?
Polya (*sharply*) All right.
Sasha (*watching*) I have to write a dissertation Papa, I was going to write about this city—but now I think I might write about an aspect of my family.

Pause

Polya (*looking up, sharply, after a pause*) You wouldn't dare? (*She suddenly moves over and starts bustling him out of the door, reluctant in his fur coat*)
Sasha (*startled*) What are you doing?
Polya Sasha was just leaving wasn't he, he's started to wear his old clothes again hasn't he? (*She pushes a startled Sasha out of the door, calling after him*) Try taking that off—and you'll freeze to death before you get to school!

Sasha exits

Polya pushes the door shut.   The band is rehearsing outside

Nikolai He is working hard, he is doing well at school.
Polya Who told you that?
Nikolai He did of course. He wouldn't lie to me.

Pause

Polya He's very eager to fit in. (*Quietly*) He'd do almost anything for that.
Nikolai (*suddenly*) Eugenia! I saw her just now, hurrying along the bridge, I must tell her how well she looks, years younger, at least ten. (*Lightly*) You must remind me to tell her, Polya—but she has no need to work.
Polya She wants to.
Nikolai She insists on doing a job! It is so utterly unnecessary. Polya, why are you so slow today?
Polya (*boiling the kettle, making tea, loudly*) Slow—I'm not being slow!
Nikolai (*lightly*) You know at the moment there is only one mechanism that

I do not fully understand—(*he smiles*)—that is the one that releases ideas, causes them to take shape. (*Charming smile*) It is becoming almost embarrassing how many ideas I have at the moment, I am being bombarded by them. Why now specially? (*Loudly*) Come on tea!

Polya Stop it. (*Loudly*) You don't yell for it anymore, remember you wait for it now.

Nikolai It seems I have little choice. Nevertheless hurry! I have a lot to do. (*After a slight pause*) I have just completed by first task, Polya. (*Calmly*) I have made moving pictures talk. I have solved the problem of amplification.

Polya (*swinging round*) I thought so ... I knew it! I guessed it was something like that, when we found the camera under here ...

Nikolai I am having some lenses made—the express order for the Northern Railway.

Polya (*excited*) Lenses! ... Are they ready?

Nikolai (*smiling, calmly*) I have told them I need the equipment urgently to record the erection of more telephone poles for posterity. Even so, they've been extremely difficult to obtain. When the lenses arrive I will be able to make some film and record the sound at the same time.

Polya You will have done it, Nikolai! (*Correcting herself*) Nikolai Semenovitch. You will have done it!

Nikolai (*calmly*) The world has been working on two approaches, racing together, sound on phonograph records matched to keep pace with the image, and sound printed directly on film—which is where the future lies.

Polya (*moving excitedly*) So, when are they coming? The emergency delivery. When can we start?

Nikolai Very soon. (*Calmly, simply*) The effect naturally will be quite devastating. For better or worse it will revolutionize popular entertainment.

Polya Yes!

Nikolai More importantly, it will alter communications—people will be able to talk to a huge audience out of the cinema screen, in a country of this size! Even quite complex ideas and information can now be spread across the continent.

Pause; he smiles

I don't want to spend my time making grandiose claims Polya—nothing could be more tiresome, nor more vulgar; but as you know, I *never* exaggerate——

Polya Once or twice, it has been known.

Nikolai Absolutely wrong—it has never been known.

Polya (*full of energy*) Where's it going to happen?

Nikolai Here of course—you will all be photographed in this carriage. (*Lightly*) The fact that the first sound film in the world will be recorded in the railway shunting yards outside Moscow ... is not my fault.

Polya (*loud*) You mean *us* on the screen—*me*! (*Suddenly her tone changes*) I am not singing any of those appalling songs you made me sing—I don't sing well enough for that for a start. If I really have to sing—it's going to be a song of my choice. (*She moves*) I might read a passage from a book. (*With a self-mocking smile*) Whatever shows me off to my best advantage.

Nikolai (*lightly*) It will be a considerable shock to the outside world, that this is coming not out of California, or Paris, or even London, but out of here—coming out of the supposed darkness of this country.

Polya (*moving backwards and forwards excited, with a spirited smile*) Will our name be on it? Will mine? In the programme ... "Polya, former domestic servant, second chamber maid, now a sorting clerk in the postal service, RECITES." Me, flickering across the screen, thirty feet high! (*She mimics flickering, jagged, movement across the screen. We suddenly see her as she would look on the screen*) All over the world. *My* voice squeaking out.

Nikolai You may well become the best remembered postal clerk in Russia. A celebrity, someone people will want to meet. (*He smiles*) I am confident nobody will realize it is a railway carriage—they will all assume it is a suite at the Hermitage so a semblance of dignity will be preserved, despite the farcical conditions in which history is being made.

Polya turns to face him

Polya It is exciting, Nikolai Semenovitch!

Nikolai Yes. Important as it is, and easily graspable for the general public though it is, it is comparatively trivial compared to what is to follow. (*He begins to move*) There is much to do, I need you for many more hours ... to redraw my diagrams, you're much neater than I am, to prepare future model work—(*he paces*)——

Polya (*stopping, her tone changing, firmly*) No! I told you I can only fit you in after work, and I can't always go on as late as you want. (*Looking straight at him*) I often won't be able to.

Pause. Nikolai looks at her

Nikolai You realize technological progress is being held up Polya, because you have to sort the grubby letters in the postal depot ... major advances, maybe halted just——

Polya I have explained to you many times why, and you still——

Nikolai (*cutting her off*) My God, Polya! How can you be so wilful and stupid.

Polya Quite easily, I'm not going to work for you when I don't want to, only when I choose. (*Suddenly loud*) Do you ever wonder why I stay, why I come back, time after time? No, you haven't, have you! Probably never crossed your mind.

A loud interrupted burst of band rehearsal outside, with sudden drumming

And how I've never doubted your work. NEVER. Though I have been kept in almost total ignorance the whole time.

Nikolai Why on earth should you have ever doubted it?

Polya Why!

Nikolai is pacing too, they are both excited

Nikolai I can't believe we're wasting time like this! . . . I can't negotiate with you Polya, there's too much to think about. (*Suddenly he stops, his tone changes*) I will continue your reading lessons, I will complete your studies, make sure you can read fluently.

Polya (*furious, fiery*) I've been able to read for ages! Books this thick! You mean you haven't noticed that? (*Loud*) No wonder you haven't mentioned it! (*Loud, moving*) I could become a professor at a university and you still wouldn't see any difference.

Nikolai I never thought you'd become so temperamental, Polya—so ridiculously pleased with yourself for some reason—and at such an inappropriate time!

Polya Me! I *am*—I'm being temperamental? (*She stops, loud*) Why shouldn't I be anyway!

Nikolai suddenly stops in the middle of the carriage

Nikolai I will do it without you! This time I will! Why should I wait for heaven's sake? (*He pauses*) I can't do it without you. There're certain things I cannot do. A few. (*He pauses*) How do you want me to ask you?

Polya (*looking at him*) We'll do it together. (*Sharply*) All right. But on my terms—(*a slight smile*)—you're not paying me after all.

Nikolai If I could explain to you what there is at stake—it is far more than talking film.

Polya Why don't you try telling me? Take the risk, I might even surprise you . . .

Nikolai It is too technical for you. (*He moves the width of the carriage*)

A solitary bell starts clanging in the distance

(*Sharply, as he moves*) I'm working on ways of advancing the use of radio, making it far more accessible, ideas that have major implications for industry, and also, a by-product of the same idea, help the deaf . . .

Suddenly the band who have been making the noise outside the carriage, break into the full, uninterrupted tune of the piece they have been rehearsing. It is a loud, stirring but mournful funeral march. Behind the noise we can hear now many more bells clanging out. Both Nikolai and Polya turn towards the windows. A moment's silence as they are surprised by the noise; they are still

My God what a noise. What's that for? Why can't they do that somewhere else?

Polya (*by the window, loud*) They seem to have got it right at last. (*Calling out*) About bloody time! It's a funeral march. (*She turns and faces Nikolai*) Who do you think can have died.

Pause. The band play the march. Nikolai draws the blinds down on the windows of the carriage as the bells rasp out

Nikolai (*turning towards her*) Polya—we must to work now.

Black-out

SCENE 2

Moscow Railway Shunting Yards. Some weeks later

The music of the band and the rasping bells break into the noise of other trains moving round the carriage, clanking close, sound of major movements, loud noises, then into silence

Sasha, now back in his grey coat, enters the darkened carriage

In the middle of the carriage, standing where the bath was, is a large unopened packing case. Sasha approaches it; he is unaware there is a figure sitting in the dark at the end of the carriage

Sasha (*starting, letting out a cry*) Comrade—I didn't see you, I didn't know we were expecting you.

Verkoff remains seated in the dark

Verkoff You weren't. (*Staring across*) I must see your father at once, it is exceptionally urgent.

Sasha My father's not here, as you can see.

Verkoff Where is he?

Sasha I don't know, comrade.

Verkoff (*loudly*) You have to know. (*He gets up, moving about the carriage, sharp movements, opening the blinds to let more light in*) What happened to my letter?—It must have arrived—(*loudly*)—it *has* arrived hasn't it?

Sasha I am sure it has, comrade ... my father tends to get a little behind with his correspondence—because he often throws letters away, but he will get better I assure you ...

Verkoff (*shouting*) You're not telling me he hasn't read it. (*Straight at him*) Has he read it or not?

Sasha I don't know, comrade.

Verkoff You better find out.

A pale, blank stare from Sasha

Who's been here?

Sasha How do you mean comrade?

Verkoff Has anybody visited here in the past weeks—been poking around, looking at things, asking you questions!

Sasha I don't think so comrade.

Verkoff (*sharply*) Don't look away like that—look at me, come on tell me, what did they say? What did they want?

Sasha (*startled by his intensity*) Nothing ... there was nobody here, comrade.

Verkoff Don't you lie to me. (*Half mock threatening, half real*) It can have terrifying consequences do you understand me. (*He pauses, a slight smile*) You *should* be afraid of me now.

Sasha You know I'd tell you at once, comrade—if there was anything to tell.

Verkoff We shall see. (*He turns towards the packing case*) What is this?

Sasha That? (*Thinking quickly*) Railway business sir, some supplies my father was just checking on, he's been waiting for them since just before the night comrade Lenin died.

Verkoff (*pushing the case*) Don't be ridiculous, this is not railway supplies. (*Loudly*) What did I just tell you? (*He looks round for something to open it with—picks up one of Nikolai's sticks, prises the top off*)

Sasha He talks more and more railway business comrade.

Verkoff (*getting the top off, looking down inside, picking one of the lenses up gingerly*) So this is what he's been up to! (*Looking at the clutter of Nikolai's work things*) I knew I was right about him—sometimes I wondered I admit. But I knew I was right!

Sasha Just a hobby, just a game of his.

Verkoff Shut up, be *quiet*. Stand over there where I can see you. Go on. (*Looking down at the work things*) I should have moved him earlier! (*Moving, looking at everything*) When I first saw you all, together, that first day in the country, standing in here, like relics from some Imperial Ball but looking pale and bloody terrified. Afraid to touch the sides in case you caught something, and pretending you weren't hungry at all, when in fact you were so starving you could have eaten each other—you were about to begin—(*a slight smile*)—weren't you?

Sasha (*hesitating, unsure of Verkoff's tone*) Almost, comrade.

Verkoff (*moving, loudly*) I won't meet someone like your father again—the Jew so obsessed with his personal appearance, wrapping himself in the finest of everything, incapable of any form of political discussion, and then ... (*Looking down into the packing case*) Look at this! (*He moves. Loudly*) I *knew* I was correct about him!

Sasha (*suddenly*) I don't think you are correct about him, comrade. My father is getting better. I know he's been neglectful, deviant, sometimes he's made me almost die of shame, but he will do his job, it takes a long time with him—to change him, to teach him.

Verkoff (*loudly*) You're going to teach him are you! (*He pauses, he turns*) You realize what I've done?

Sasha Yes.

Verkoff What do you mean "yes"? You don't have to give a blind sychophantic yelp to everything I say.

Sasha (*after a pause*) Yes, comrade.

Verkoff (*suddenly exuberantly, lightly*) What I've done is incredibly important——

Sasha I know.

Verkoff My job—the job I am doing—people could look at it in years to come and see what looks like simple bureaucratic organization, railways, telephone exchanges, drains, it might seem tedious, routine, mere clockwork—in truth the work was *fantastic*. You know why?

Sasha Why comrade?

Verkoff Because I used my imagination—in a thousand different opportunities, small things, and major ones, I made some surprising decisions—every case was different, every case on its merits. (*He smiles*) It was an inspired burst of planning.

Sasha Yes I know——

Verkoff (*with a wry smile*) And who is going to remember an obscure official, tell me—one of the ministers of labour, of public works . . .

Sasha They will, comrade.

Verkoff (*lightly*) People will always remember the obvious figures natur- ally—everyone else gets bludgeoned on to the sidelines. Forgotten! (*A slight smile*) But that is not the way things actually happen at the time. They will never realize what I did! That my department is spectacularly successful. Does it matter?—it matters like hell to me at the moment. (*Suddenly sharp*) And I can assure you I intend to keep it as long as possible. I'm certainly not done yet!

Pause. Sasha stares at him

What a blank look that is.

Pause

Your ignorance frightens me, boy. (*Staring at the pale face of the teenage boy*) You're as bad as them do you know that—you have to be told what you ought to think, have to be absolutely sure what the correct thing to say is before you dare open your mouth.

Sasha stares at him

The physical effort required to talk to people who only deal in certainties, you have no idea! It's so bloody tiring! (*Pulling him closer*) Come here—so who was it that came here, come on tell me, I know somebody was.

Sasha No sir. They haven't, I promise you.

Verkoff (*with a slight smile*) Just checking, I'm not at all sure I believe you . . . (*He pauses, staring at the boy*) The furniture has suddenly been changed in my office.

Sasha Has it, comrade—is it an improvement?

Verkoff (*with a shrewd look*) We shall see . . . now listen to me carefully, so there is no possibility of error, I'm instructing you to leave the country— and this instruction has to be obeyed in the next few days!

Sasha (*stunned*) Leave the country? What do you mean?

Verkoff That's what you have to do. (*He scrawls a one-line note on a scrap of paper, and leaves it on the side*)

Sasha Has Papa been that negligent? I told you he will get better—he will do his duties . . .

Verkoff (*lightly*) I will put it very simply so it can be intelligible even to you—it is a small matter of life and death.

Sasha Life and death?

Verkoff For all of you.

Sasha All of us?

Verkoff Those are my orders to you. And find that letter! (*He moves*) If you ever get to the border that letter might make it a great deal easier for you to leave. (*He pauses*) Or it might not.

Sasha (*worried*) That isn't very clear comrade, if I may say so . . .

Verkoff I must go! I have so many people to see. (*Suddenly looking down at his clothes at the door*) Good God, I'm covered in mud, I never noticed, why didn't you tell me? Didn't you see? (*A sharp smile*) Because it's a form of uniform you never noticed! (*As he exits*) You know what you have to do, you have to try and leave.

Verkoff exits

Sasha (*moving over to the door, calling after him*) But he won't go—he won't go until he's finished his work, comrade. (*He shouts, close by the door*) What am *I* meant to do—he won't listen to me he can't be made to stop don't you realize, he won't stop his "*work*" don't you see! (*Turning back to the carriage*) How can I do anything? . . . (*He breaks off— staring at the box in the middle of the carriage. He lifts off the top prised open by Verkoff, he lets the top drop on to the floor*) I think whatever these are . . . (*Dipping his hands in and lifting up glass wrapped in straw, so the glass catches the light, flashes out brightly*) Whatever they happen to be—they will have to go. (*He drops the lens back on to the others in the box making a clanking noise. Staring into the box*) It has to be good enough to *stop* him. (*He picks up a hammer and a long knife from among the equipment lying in his father's corner; he moves back to the box, lifts one of the lenses again and runs the top of the knife down it—scratching its surface. Then he knocks the lens with a clean sharp hit from the hammer; it splits in two. Very pale, he stands with the hammer and a long metal bar taken from the side, staring down into the box. He chooses to do it with the hammer. Suddenly he swings it again and again into the box, it goes up above his head, and coming down with startling ferocity with each blow. A ferocious burst of destruction as he pummels the contents of the box*)

Sasha hears the sound of them approaching, Polya's voice and laughter

(*Looking around him very fast*) Better do something else . . .

Sasha runs round the length of the carriage upturning furniture, turning drawers out, tearing sheets down the middle with the long knife, slashing some of the chairs, the beds; just before Polya enters he begins to try to scratch some graffiti—a slogan on the ornamental panelling, but drops the knife and kicks it under the bunk, as Polya reaches the door. Sasha leans against the wall very still, looking pale

Polya enters, stares at the destruction

Polya (*shocked, quiet*) Sasha—what on earth has happened?

Sasha is staring from the far end of the carriage

Sasha There's been an attack—some people got in, . . . and they've done this.

Polya (*moving slowly into the carriage*) Who were they? (*She pauses*) I mean they've torn the place apart, Sasha.

Sasha I've just come back . . . I just found it, now.

Polya (*suddenly looking at him, moving close to him*) Are you all right—not hurt Sasha love—(*touching him*)—they didn't do anything to you, didn't attack you . . .

Sasha (*as she touches his face*) I just missed them ...

Polya No, nothing ... (*She withdraws, disappointed at herself for showing such warm feelings towards him*) You were very lucky. (*She looks across the carriage*) Who would have wanted to attack here?

Sasha (*suddenly*) The Commissar of Labour came—he left this note, Polya.

Polya (*looking down at the shattered glass and equipment in the box*) Oh my God—not here too. (*Picking up a broken lens. Looking very pale, suddenly moving*) Your father—what will he do? He's waited months for these. He could kill people for this, (*quietly*) so could I (*sharply*) how did they *know* this was here? (*Moving*) What can we do to lessen——

Nikolai enters with Eugenia. Nikolai immediately stops in the door, stock still

Nikolai What have you two been doing?

Eugenia (*staring around her*) Oh no Sasha, (*sharply*) who's done this?

Polya Nikolai Semenovitch prepare yourself ... there's been an attack as you can see, and—(*she stops*)

Sasha (*quietly*) There's also a note from the Commissar of Labour telling us to leave.

He holds it out and Eugenia takes it. Silence

Nikolai (*standing in the doorway pointing at the packing case with his stick calmly*) Are they all broken?

Polya Yes, they're broken.

Nikolai (*calmly*) Not just the lenses. All of it?

Polya All of it.

Pause

Nikolai (*his voice very precise, deadly calm*) I don't think that will prove too much of a problem. (*A slight pause*) All of them smashed, all broken—it doesn't present too much of a problem, no ... (*After a pause, his voice rising, suddenly dangerous*) It just means I will not be able to finish my work. (*He is very still, but the rage is beginning to pass through his body*) Those who did this have to be found—they will have to be dealt with in the only way that is fitting ...

Pause. They all stare at him

They will have to be hunted down wherever they have chosen to hide themselves and destroyed.

Eugenia (*moving, not daring to go too close to him*) Nikolai ... I know ... what's happened is a terrible shock, (*holding Verkoff's note*) but there's also this——

Nikolai cuts her off

Nikolai (*suddenly the shout coming out*) My God, why do people do such things—have this desire to smash and tear up anything they don't understand—this compulsion to stamp all over it. I hope they realize I am capable of just as much and *more*. I can be as violent as they are and more

effective. They will be found. They will be made to face what they have
done, they've tried to extinguish—four years' work——

Polya (*looking at the broken pieces*) Maybe we can . . .

Nikolai I can assure you—they will NOT succeed. I will not let them
succeed.

Pause

Eugenia My love, I'm not sure we can afford to ignore this note from the
Commissar of Labour, instructing us to leave the country, he says he sent
us a letter . . .

Nikolai takes the note, but is continuing to pace. Pause

Nikolai I will do it. That is both a promise and a warning and nothing can
stop that now. (*He pauses—a quick glance at the note*) And there is no
question of me fleeing this country.

Nikolai exits

*Both women move back and forth across the carriage automatically, picking
up the shattered pieces, trying to patch the torn interior of the carriage
together*

Eugenia Nikolai . . . (*Staring at the mess*) I knew something from the
outside would come bursting in here one day, I'm almost surprised it's
nothing worse.

Polya (*staring at the broken equipment*) It's bad enough. But he will find a
way. Whoever tried to stop him, won't.

Sasha stares, with his back to the wall

Eugenia (*loudly, suddenly*) Polya—this could just be a taste of what is to
come—do we try to stay or do we leave?

Polya I don't know.

Eugenia (*turning, determined*) We have to find that letter from the Minister
of Labour before there are any official changes, we have to use it . . .
perhaps we could use a health reason. (*She is moving up and down*) If we
decide to leave, I heard people were doing that—(*she pauses*)—we could
say something like mine or Sasha's health is unlikely to stand up to
another winter . . .

Polya (*smiling*) It's only spring now.

Eugenia (*moving*) I know!

Polya It might work . . .

Eugenia Nikolai would never agree of course.

Polya I could use your travel permits, travel with you, some of the way to
the border, and then move down south, find a new job!

Eugenia (*looking up*) You might be better off leaving at once—the danger
may be getting contagious, being with us. (*After a slight pause*) I don't
know, Polya, I would never forgive myself if something happened to you
because of us.

Polya You've got to *tell* him, Eugenia, whatever you decide . . . it's your
future too.

Sasha (*watching them*) Polya would stay with us as long as possible.
Polya So you want that now, do you? What for?
Sasha We'll need your advice.
Polya Really. The problem is I don't like you very much at the moment, Sasha. Remember?
Sasha That doesn't matter now.

Pause. Polya stares at him

Polya Speak for yourself.

Black-out

SCENE 3

The carriage at the border. Some time later. Night

The sound of movement, of trains passing very close, loud braking noises, the wrenching of metal, feeling of large important movements of people, of machines, in the night. Voices calling sporadically in the distance, phones ringing and stopping and ringing again, a sense of contained chaos. The noise punctuated by bouts of silence. The sounds continue to erupt again from time to time, close to them, brushing right up to them, near the window

Sasha and Eugenia, Polya, Nikolai are altogether in the carriage. It is night, the packing cases have been pushed back into a corner—the pigskin luggage is splayed all over the carriage half open, but most of their possessions are still around the carriage. Eugenia is moving with clothes. Polya lifts the blind of one of the windows to stare out, a passing light stabs through at them and is gone. Their mood is tense but excited, Nikolai sitting calmly in the middle of them all. Polya pulls the blind right up

Eugenia What can you see, Polya?
Polya Somebody holding a fluffy dog out of another train window so it can pee.
Sasha (*by the other window*) Just blackness here, there's that ringing all the time—I can't see from where. (*He jumps up by the window, climbing up*)

Incessant ringing continues in the distance

Polya It's one of the telephones ringing in the guard posts by the other platforms—nobody ever seems to answer it.
Eugenia We've got here anyway—I never thought we'd do it. (*She turns*) We probably shouldn't have given our passes to those young soldiers—we should have kept them with us.
Polya They were friendly enough. (*With a sharp smile. She moves*) There're so many trains here, going back in all directions, I'm spoiled for choice, which one I take to the South.
Eugenia (*quietly*) I keep thinking you ought to have got off earlier, Polya... (*Moving*) You will remember, Nikolai, you're not going to talk about your work to them—or even much about your job for the Government. The less we say the better—we're not going to tell the *whole* truth.
Nikolai (*calmly*) I remember, yes.

There is noise close by

Polya (*sharply by the window*) Did you see they were letting no-one stay on the platform—people sitting and sleeping on the bank along the line for about three miles.

Eugenia And they seemed to have dropped their belongings everywhere, all over the rails, a lot of people do it on purpose I think—getting rid of valuables they think they better not risk.

Polya (*climbing up by the window, straining to see*) Yes, you can just see back there, on that huge pile of coal by the line, it's shining with all the things they've thrown out of the windows, people's silver ...

Eugenia Thank God we got rid of ours, and the firearms too.

Nikolai is sitting calmly in the middle

Polya (*to Sasha*) Are you going to do well—do what you have to do?

Sasha I think so.

Eugenia (*with a nervous smile*) Does he look pale enough do you think? And we still haven't found that letter from the Minister of Labour.

Polya His cheeks are blooming of course—(*to Sasha*)—try to make you look ill and you seem to get healthier by the minute, never seen you look so well! Come on, let's hear you cough; harder, COUGH.

Sasha I am coughing!

Nikolai (*quietly*) That won't be necessary.

Polya (*touching Sasha*) I haven't liked you for many months you know, not until the last few days.

Sasha Polya—there's something I did, I'll have to tell you one day.

The door opens, Guard 1 and Guard 2 enter. They are dressed in heavy coats, new uniforms, very bulky in the confined space. They look totally different, almost unrecognizable, older, more haggard. The small stocky Guard 2 is much less exuberant, much more deferential to the younger Guard 1, who is more efficient, confident, authoritative. They show no sign of recognizing Nikolai, their manner brisk from having had to process so many people

Guard 1 (*looking at his clipboard, then at the passengers grouped at one end of the carriage*) These your papers here ... Nikolai Pesiakoff ...

Nikolai Yes ... (*For the first time his manner is unsure, not certain how to dissemble*) As you can see they are clear, everything is self-explanatory, there is no problem.

Guard 1 (*looking down at the papers*) Destination London, via Berlin ... that certainly is clear enough. Three travel permits.

Eugenia (*sharply*) Yes!

Guard 1 (*looking at Polya*) What are you doing here?

Polya I'm not staying with them, I'm just a friend, I am here to change trains.

Nikolai (*suddenly looking straight at the guards*) What are your names?

Guard 1 Our names? That need not concern you—(*looking at him*)—allow us to ask the questions.

Nikolai I am almost certain, I don't think I'm wrong, we have met before. At another station, much smaller than this one, somewhere along that vast bleak stretch of the Northern Railway, which at one time I had to move up and down.

Guard 1 (*calmly*) I can assure you we have never met before. (*Moving with papers*) Now what are your reasons for wishing to travel outside the country, comrade?

Eugenia The reasons are on our papers, it's all set down, we told the other guards.

Guard 1 (*calmly*) I know what your papers say—but I want to hear your version. (*Staring at them*)

Nikolai You want me to tell you?

Pause

The reasons we are leaving, I mean we're travelling . . . I am escorting my family out of the country because . . . (*He stops*) We have obtained permission because . . . (*He falters, finding it difficult to lie*) Because my son's health is . . . because when, if the winter is, when the winter . . . (*He stops*)

Eugenia My husband has had a long journey, please remember . . .

Nikolai Because my son must . . .

Sasha Papa, I will tell them . . .

Nikolai No!

Pause

I am not going to go on with this, it is an unbelievable excuse, I am not going to lie to you, I have not had enough practice for one thing and do it poorly, and it insults your intelligence. (*He looks straight at the guards*) I am Nikolai Polyapoff. I am taking my family across the border and then I will be returning almost immediately—in time we will all return I assure you. I am appointed the Telephone Examiner of the Northern District— this carriage has been made available for my use.

Pause; they are all watching him

More importantly I have some vital work to complete which should prove of some use. (*He pauses*) I will be ordering some new components and equipment from abroad and returning, so you see you have merely to rubber stamp our permits, it is all a formality. Moreover, I am certain you must remember this now, I recommended you two for promotion when we stumbled across each other, in exchange for some help you gave me in finding some equipment for my work. (*He smiles*) It happens to be one of the few official letters I ever wrote.

Silence. The guards watch him

Guard 1 I have been very patient . . .

Guard 2 You are trying to tell us you were the Telephone Surveyor of the Northern Railway.

Nikolai Of course.

Guard 2 (*loudly*) That is not true.

Guard 1 (*moving round the carriage, looking at everything, his manner methodical, but sharp*) It is certainly not true. I did meet him. I can't remember it all, it was some time ago, and a *great deal* has happened since then, but one thing I know for certain, he could have been nothing like you.

Guard 2 I remember him a bit, he arrived out of the night, and he was nothing like you—(*sharp, party manner*)—a very conscientious official. *Punctillious*.

Nikolai (*calmly*) That person was I—it seems odd that it is you who look different and not me, but I recognize you. (*Lightly*) I recommended you for a position of increased responsibility, it appears to have worked almost too well.

Guard 2 (*loudly*) You're not him, all right? No influence was used in getting us where we are, either.

Guard 2 begins a search of the carriage

Eugenia (*sharply*) What's he doing?

Nikolai Who do you think I am then? How else could I possibly be in this—(*indicating the carriage*)—and have got it joined to a train coming to the border?

Guard 1 (*very incisive, suddenly we see how overworked and tense he is*) My God—don't waste my time, we have people arriving here in all sorts of ways, all forms of transport, having bribed, cajoled, sometimes killed, to get here—even just to get a compartment to themselves.

As Guard 2 searches

And we have to deal with them all. People being arrogant or worse, obsequious, people trying to squeeze through holes that haven't been plugged, before it's too late. Pushing, refusing to wait, shouting out and complaining all night, grabbing hold of your arm, poking you in the face with their sticks.

Guard 2 Last night somebody shouted at me—what I thought was a frail old man, he screamed, "I don't expect you've ever seen a golf club before you ignorant fool", he then lifted it above his head and smashed it through the air at me. (*He demonstrates. Then turning to Eugenia, he hands her some letters he's uncovered*). Are these yours?

Eugenia (*grabbing them*) Yes.

Guard 1 (*looking at Nikolai*) And the lies we have to deal with too, people producing whole new histories for themselves.

Guard 2 Some of them don't pretend at all but *demand* to be let out at *once*.

Guard 1 (*quiet, strong*) Desperate to leave the land of their birth—the country is disgorging people at the moment, the waste that didn't leave before is finally leaving now. Some of it can be allowed to drain out, others have to stay because of what they've done. (*He moves*) We have lists, and we can't afford to make mistakes.

The phone rings in the background

That telephone never ever stops ringing with news, instructions. Of all the teams working here, we are the team being held responsible.

Guard 2 I have never worked so hard in my entire life!

Nikolai (*calmly*) You will remember me.

Guard 2 suddenly moves across the carriage, having found a package in a silk bag

Guard 2 Look at this. (*He hands it to Guard 1*)

Guard 1 holds the silk bag

Guard 1 Can you explain these, comrade?

Nikolai (*calmly*) They are diamonds.

Eugenia (*surprised by this find, but immediately recovering*) We were *allowed* to take some diamonds out, family possessions, we——

Guard 1 Nobody is allowed to take such things as diamonds out of the country—(*staring at them*)—why weren't they on your form? Among your papers.

Eugenia (*sharply*) There's so much to write down, somehow they got left out.

Guard 1 You left out diamonds?

Polya They would have been better hidden if we'd intended to hide them, wouldn't they?

Nikolai (*calmly*) They were not hidden in any way, I would never allow that.

Guard 1 (*staring at them*) None of you must now leave this carriage, for any reason. You will remain here.

Pause

If you are right and you sought permission, which was granted, this will be the first time this has happened. If you're wrong—the consequences could be grave. (*Moving to exit*) We will have to make a telephone call. We will see.

Guard 1 and Guard 2 exit

Eugenia (*loudly*) Why did you keep those, Nikolai—why on earth did you bring the diamonds with us. (*She looks at him*) I thought we had got rid of everything.

Nikolai I wanted you to have security abroad when I had to leave you, some source of income. (*He pauses; lightly*) Perhaps you should have been wearing them—we should have been even more straightforward.

Eugenia Whatever the reason, that wasn't wise Nikolai . . .

Nikolai Don't worry—at the worst they will attempt to confiscate them.

Eugenia starts looking through the unopened letters the guard found

He couldn't remember me, the guard. He was not lying, I don't blame him he is quite busy he was thinking how I must have looked in retrospect— slightly nervous of the truth, so he simply altered it. He'll remember.

Eugenia (*looking up sharply*) This is *the* letter Nikolai, the Minister of Labour's letter.

Polya It's found!

Nikolai What does he say? Is it of any use to us?

Eugenia (*staring down at the first page of the letter, eager*) He says ... he says ... my God!

Polya What?

Eugenia (*reading*) "When you first came into my office with all those ideas—this ludicrous even grotesque figure, I had to restrain my clerks from tearing you to pieces—but your *ideas*, your papers you submitted? I didn't understand them—but they were extraordinary——"

Sasha (*surprised*) Extraordinary?

Eugenia (*carrying straight on*) "—despite the fact that they were written on notepaper from the Ritz Hotel in Paris! You certainly didn't look a likely inventor of anything—could such modern notions which would actually work be churning around in such a person? The answer was *yes* ... maybe, perhaps. The trouble was if I gave you space to work in Moscow people would literally probably strangle you inside a week."

Nikolai Proceed.

Eugenia (*excited*) I can't believe this. (*She reads*) "I had an inspiration! One of the many I had at the time—*I will make him Telephone Examiner before there is any real need for one.*"

Polya What! (*Reading over her shoulder*) "I will give him a place of his own, a Government appointment that will protect him, access to labour and funds if he chooses to use them."

Eugenia "I knew you wouldn't do a stroke of railway work—as it is I received some delightful lies from your wife—" (*She breaks off*) He might have told me mightn't he! (*She returns to the letter*) "—some of which are on my wall staring at me now."

Polya Yes, yes, why didn't he let *us* know?

Sasha suddenly grabs the second page of the letter and starts to read from the top of the page

Sasha "I knew if you succeeded Nikolai, you would break every door down in Moscow to show people—if you failed, if you were a fraud, I could just write it off as railway expense." (*Reading fast, agitated, realizing his own grave mistake*) "And Nikolai, I knew if I told you the *truth* you wouldn't stand it for a moment and would be camping on a doorstep, refusing to go, telling my staff they weren't dressed properly, that they were all ignorant peasants! *So*, you got put in the carriage—*and it is just beginning, I hope, to bear some sort of fruit.*" (*To himself*) Oh! "I have to break off in a hurry, I have other urgent letters to write."

Nikolai (*loudly*) Give me that letter!

Sasha (*moving away*) What have I done? ... Polya, you don't know what I've done. I've been so stupid, didn't see anything. I have done something terrible, truly terrible.

Polya (*concerned*) What's the matter with you?

Nikolai (*commanding*) Sasha quiet . . .

Silence. Nikolai takes the letter

(*Calmly*) The idiot—why didn't he explain this to me, he treated me like a child. (*Calmly*) I fail to understand the use of "ludicrous" and "grotesque" . . . and he seems almost as vain as I am.

Pause

Nevertheless he could have done worse—it is true he could have done much worse.

Eugenia (*with feeling*) Yes.

Nikolai There was a mind at work there, an intelligence. (*With a slight smile*) He enjoyed my contradictions. (*Lightly*) It might even be a document of historical interest—all the more reason to complete the task.

Polya (*with a tense smile*) And you can still do it with *me*, which is important, still got the chance. (*Moving, febrile, by the window*) Find some new equipment round here and as the first talking film you can have me singing at the border. Wailing out of a window!

Nikolai Yes.

There is the sound of movement outside

Polya You can use some of the people outside, the people queuing, and the guards, you can have them all telling their stories, record the faces and shouts from the border . . .

Nikolai (*with a slight smile*) Finding the equipment here Polya, is slightly unlikely but this—(*holding the Minister of Labour's letter*)—this is a splendid find, we have no problem now. We just give them the letter—it shows who I am—it is a proof of everything.

Eugenia I don't think that would be wise. (*She takes the letter*)

Nikolai Why, how can it not be?

Eugenia We don't know where he is now—what has happened to him. Until we know that, I'm not sure anyone should read it. (*She glances down at the letter*)

The door opens suddenly; Guard 2 enters

Nikolai You have brought our papers now I hope.

Guard 2 (*pointing straight at Polya*) Right, she has to leave, come on get your things and *out.*

Polya Me? (*After a startled pause*) Why now?

Guard 2 You don't get to ask questions, you do as you're told. You've got to leave, so you get up, take a few things, and you get out of here!

Polya I will leave how I like, in my own time.

Guard 2 (*shouting*) Don't play around with me—I haven't slept for three nights, you realize, and it's getting worse all the time, it never ever stops——

Phones and noise in the background

So don't you try arguing.

Eugenia lifts her head

The rest of you keep quiet!

Polya (*moving deliberately over to Sasha*) Sasha, despite everything—(*she gives him a kiss, slightly formal*)—I think I might even miss you. (*Then turning, instinctively reverting to her former role for a second, checking clothes*) You know where all your winter clothes are—in which suitcase, where the thick socks are?

Sasha (*moving after her*) Polya, you're not still angry with me? (*Loudly*) You're not to be. I wanted so much to belong, that's all—wanted to be part of things, what was happening . . .

Polya (*looking at him again*) Yes, I know.

Sasha (*quietly*) And all the time it seems I was nearer to it than I thought, Papa's work . . .

Guard 2 I told you to get a move on . . .

Sasha One day I'll tell you what I did . . . when things are easier I'll . . .

Polya When that happens, I'll want to hear it.

Sasha I destroyed something, Polya.

Polya (*touching him*) Worry about things in the past later, you've got to be strong now, Sasha.

Guard 2 (*suddenly turning to Nikolai*) Right, now you, take that coat off and give it to me.

Pause

Nikolai For any particular reason?

Guard 2 Just do as I say—everything will be much simpler if you do that.

Nikolai (*calmly, taking the greatcoat off*) Do I get a receipt?

Eugenia What are you doing? What's happening?

Guard 2 (*to Nikolai*) Now the jacket, and the shirt, go on give them to me. (*To Eugenia*) Your husband is shortly going to be removed from this carriage, he will be charged tonight, and taken away from here for sentence.

Polya (*loudly*) Why?

Eugenia Where's the trial? Where's he going?

Guard 2 (*cutting her off*) You and the child are forbidden to stay, you continue out of the country tonight (*sharply*) you understand? (*To Nikolai*) Now take your shoes. (*Pointing at his polished feet*) Fine shoes there, take them off, and your socks, off!

Nikolai hesitates

I don't want to hurt anybody, but there's an allocated time for each person, so just do it.

Nikolai I have no intention of running away. (*Nikolai obeys instructions. Without his magnificent coat, gloves, hat, the jacket of his suit, his shirt he is left in his vest and trousers, barefoot, looking frail and vulnerable, suddenly older, whiter, but he is sitting very straight, in the middle of the carriage*)

Polya (*watching Nikolai undress*) You don't have do do that do him . . .

Guard 2 (*looking at Polya and her papers*) Why on earth did you bother staying with this lot anyway? Cleaning up after them, running around ... why?

Polya (*facing him*) So you're allowed to ask questions and I'm not.

Eugenia (*warning*) Polya ...

Guard 2 Why?

Polya I did it for my own reasons, because *I* wanted to. Because I was doing something important here with him.

Guard 2 looks disbelieving

(*Indicating Nikolai*) Yes, *with* him. One way and another a lot of me had gone into it, it was *my* work as well as his. (*With feeling*) And I really did want to see it through, more than you can imagine. And we've just reached a point, as it happens, when ...

The telephone rings outside

Guard 2 There's that phone. Come on, get ready now! (*Holding the fur coat; to Nikolai*) That's more like it.

Nikolai (*calmly, to the women*) It is all right. This is only very temporary.

Guard 2 Everything out of the pockets, empty the pockets. (*He shouts through window at the ringing phone*) Stop that ringing for God's sake, answer the bloody thing.

Polya (*loud, powerful*) He'll die the death of cold—I haven't spent this time with him—to see him wiped out by pneumonia. (*Turning*) What harm has he done, what harm could he possibly do?

Eugenia (*warning*) Polya ...

Guard 2 We're finding out a lot more about him now—information is still coming through from Moscow. (*To Polya*) Now have you got what you want—otherwise you will leave with nothing. (*Looking round the carriage*)

Polya (*loudly*) And stop ferreting around—there is nothing else to find.

Nikolai Polya ... there is no need for that.

Polya (*facing him*) I've known each of these poeple for years—it is not possible to say goodbye in a few seconds and I won't ...

Guard 2 (*briskly, not unpleasantly*) You get extremely used to seeing people do it, all ages, all kinds of relationships, it's much simpler this way I can assure you.

Polya (*to Nikolai*) They will realize they are making a mistake.

Nikolai Naturally. I will be returning ready to resume very soon, Polya. (*To Guard 2*) Some heating here would now be appreciated.

Guard 2 No chance, this is no longer a hotel. (*Really tense*) Don't give me any more trouble, all right?

Polya (*up to her*) Eugenia ...

Eugenia (*touching her*) I don't know how I will live without seeing you.

Polya You'll manage—you know where everything is.

Eugenia I didn't mean that, (*worried*) you know I didn't mean about domestic things Polya, I——

Guard 2 (*breaking in, pulling Polya by the arm*) Come on, that's enough.

Polya (*back to Eugenia*) Of course I . . . (*Fighting the guard*) Stop it, stop
that.

*The guard is grabbing at her, short sharp grabs at her, she fights him off, till
he's really got her, suddenly she's dragged out the carriage very forcibly and
gone*

Eugenia She's left and I didn't make myself clear what I meant. (*She moves,
loudly*) She's gone and she thought I was talking about domestic work.

*Polya appears, framed in one of the windows, staring back at them looking
startled, pale, as there is the sound of the door being fastened from the
outside. Then she is forcibly moved away, telephones ringing in the distance*

Nikolai Polya . . .

Eugenia Why are they being so rough with her? They'll let her get her train,
won't they?

Nikolai Yes, they will.

Eugenia (*to Nikolai*) What are they going to do, how will they treat *you*?

Nikolai There will be no further problems—they won't seriously attempt to
detain me. (*After a pause*) My feet are cold that's all. (*Sitting in his vest,
carrying on as if nothing had happened*) It may be difficult though for me
to return here to Russia—for some time.

Pause

(*Acidly*) What a destination! What a fate. To end up in England!

Eugenia I thought that's what you've always wished for, above all.

Nikolai (*astonished*) Always wished for! (*After a pause*) The idea horrifies
me. (*With a self-mocking smile*) When I went there I had an utterly
miserable time, grey and utterly sodden. They're terribly slow the English,
you have to explain everything so many times, they think in such a literal
way. It is all so rigid there, they treat their servants appallingly.
(*Incisively*) There is no energy of ideas, they instinctively distrust nearly
all ideas on sight, and they like you to apologize for having thought of
them. They thought I was mad and exceedingly arrogant, they backed
away from me when I came into the room, always looked at their feet.
They have a terror of everything foreign. (*Lightly*) They will not believe in
me, this "grotesque" did not and will not go down well. (*With a slight
smile*) Also, and even more important, the coffee is disgusting, undrink-
able.

Eugenia You never told me—you never told me that's what happened.

The sound of movement around them

Nikolai No, and we haven't got the money to reach America—(*with a slight
smile*)—might be worse of course. (*His tone changing*) It is interesting isn't
it, nothing I have ever read or been told in my life has prepared me for this
shock, the sheer physical sensation when one is faced with leaving one's
native land permanently—like being pulled away from a magnetic field
and that everything will then stop.

Eugenia I know, I can feel it. I'm not sure that's all that's going to happen,
Nikolai. (*She puts a blanket round him*)

Nikolai If they were going to shoot me—they would have probably done it already. But it's such a remote possibility, don't worry about it my dear.
Eugenia (*suddenly sharp*) Nikolai, we both know what they're going to do. (*Loudly*) Let's not pretend, all right.

Pause; she looks across at him

(*Loudly*) Why didn't you tell me ever?
Nikolai Tell you what?
Eugenia Tell me what you were doing—what your work was. I heard it from Polya—all these ideas—(*looking at him*)—didn't I have a right to know?
Nikolai I did not discuss such things with you . . . you knew that.
Eugenia (*her head going back, quietly*) Yes I knew that.

They're sitting wide apart in the carriage, Sasha crouching, in the corner, the phones ringing in the distance

I didn't know how long we've got—when they're going to come back, maybe in the middle. (*Tracing a pattern on the wall with her finger not looking at him*) I have no idea if I can go through with this . . . but if I don't say it now I'm never going to be able to say it. (*Tension is in her voice, trying to keep control*)

Nikolai Eugenia what is it?
Eugenia (*with real force suddenly*) I want you to realize what it was like Nikolai before, our lives together. Before we came here. (*Forcing herself to say it*) What it meant for me . . . how . . . how—(*forcing herself*)—how I had to support and not ask, (*not looking at him*) give to you but never touch, serve (*quieter*) but never ever . . . demand.
Nikolai (*cutting her off*) I don't know you should say these things now—the boy is here, Sasha is here.
Eugenia I have to, Kolia—I have to tell you. (*Quietly with feeling*) But it isn't easy. (*Not looking at him*) Your work—this enormous weight in the air always, a world I was forbidden to enter . . . but for some reason I always believed in it, I don't doubt it for a moment, I know it's real. But my God, when you left me in the country how I hated those summers, those horrible summers, endless languid days and how I *hated* you sometimes. (*A momentary look at him*) Yes.
Nikolai (*looking up*) Hated me? Eugenia . . .
Eugenia (*with feeling*) I could hardly think for myself. Waiting for you . . . all the time waiting for you to *see* me, to discuss with me, ANYTHING, to *acknowledge* me. If I ever have to live through that again with me festering underneath (*matter of fact*) beginning to scream and cry inside . . . (*holding herself*) I felt there was so much in here . . . trapped in here . . . it was like burrowing out of a grave. Nikolai, forgive me. (*After a pause*)

But . . . (*She stops*)
Nikolai Go on, proceed. Say what you have to say.
Eugenia (*who has looked up, is staring at him*) This is the most difficult conversation of my life—if I look at you I can't go on. (*Trying to keep control—after waivering, her voice incisive again*) But if I don't try to do it

I won't be able to cope afterwards at all. (*She turns away leaning against the side. Forcing herself to go on*) It's just the daring it took to break with all I'd thought before—and do the few things I did, forging documents, making up train times, tiny little acts which led to my getting that job . . . absurd as it may seem now they were terribly important at the time, the release I felt doing that it was extraordinarily strong—that welled up because of that. (*She looks up again*) What I am trying to tell you is, though you seem to have been completely oblivious of it over these last months . . . (*she pauses*) But it changed my life Nikolai, I want you to understand that—(*she pauses*)—because otherwise . . . if you go away now . . . I feel there're things we never said . . . and then . . . (*She stops*) Oh Nikolai, say something, help me . . .

Silence

Nikolai (*in a detached tone*) It is very interesting I think . . .
Eugenia What is! Is that all you can say? (*Sharply*) At this time.
Nikolai (*continuing, not looking at her*) Large events, great events even, have happened just outside, and we've seen most of them—or heard most of them to be more accurate. Meanwhile in here, locked up in this, squashed into this matchbox.
Eugenia Rather a large matchbox, Nikolai.
Nikolai (*continuing, detached tones*) And yet the energy generated in here. It seems to me Eugenia, in this messy clump of all of us, all of us tangled up together, a way was found of releasing our separate energies—(*he pauses*)—unlocking things.
Eugenia (*not looking at him, sharply*) That's how you'd put it is it?
Nikolai (*slowly*) And I know some of that . . . (*staring at her*) . . . a lot of that is because of you.

Silence, Eugenia looks up

Eugenia Yes it is. (*She looks at him*) And Polya.
Nikolai (*staring at her*) Just because I find certain things difficult to say doesn't mean they aren't true. (*After a slight pause*) I've been meaning to say many things to you.
Eugenia Yes.
Nikolai (*with a slight smile*) And you know before this I never could think on trains—I never had an idea on one in my life.
Eugenia Kolia, is there anything we can do when they come?
Nikolai No.
Sasha Papa, I'm so sorry, I am. I am so sorry, Papa.
Nikolai Yes. But there's no need for that. (*In a detached tone*) You know I never thought waiting for one's possible execution one's mind would be so clear, it's a pleasant surprise. It's *interesting* to find that——
Eugenia (*suddenly moving over to him, touching him*) Kolia don't say that any more. Look at me. You don't have to talk like that. (*Touching him*) I can't believe I may have to say goodbye to you. (*Looking at him*) I'm deliberately refusing to try.

The door bangs open. Guards 1 and 2 enter

Nikolai (*calmly*) So here you are, you left rather suddenly, I didn't know whether you were coming back.

Guard 1 Nikolai Pesiakoff you are under arrest—you have to come with us now. You may bring no personal belongings.

Guard 2 Don't cause us trouble, you've had time to say goodbye by now.

Nikolai What is the charge?

Guard 1 Apart from trying to remove valuables unlawfully from this country, you have lied about being a Government official, both are capital offences.

Guard 2 The Minister of Labour you referred to, they'd never heard of him when we telephoned! We told them to look again, they think he's been arrested.

Guard 1 (*to Nikolai*) Right, stand up—time to move.

Eugenia (*staring up*) You going to try to take him just like that are you? No shoes.

Guard 2 That's how we have to do it.

Eugenia (*suddenly*) How dare you treat somebody like that—how dare you touch him.

Guard 1 Don't try to get yourself arrested as well—it is not something I want to have to do.

Eugenia And how dare you not believe me. (*Staring at them*) Didn't you hear him tell you what he did—he worked for the Northern Railway.

Sasha He did!

Guard 1 He could never have——

Eugenia (*cutting him off*) We wouldn't make up such a mad lie.

Guard 1 Many do.

Eugenia How do you *know* he's not? I'll prove it to you. (*Sharply, keeping her eyes on them*) Do you know who the station master is for instance at Vologda, come on who is he? Tell me. Sergei Goncharov—(*before they can stop her*)—or do you know for instance what is now different about the train from Omsk to Moscow, have either of you any idea?

Guard 1 (*watching her, intrigued*) No.

Eugenia Of course you don't—it is the first time a through express train has ever been run on that line, it's being run for an experimental period of three months.

Guard 1 (*with an intrigued smile*) An uncommon sight—a woman spouting railway statistics from the heart!

Eugenia Don't you patronize me, comrade. (*Staring at him*) When is the delivery expected of the new locomotives the ones built entirely in this country—October thirty-first.

Guard 2 (*disbelieving*) Really?

Eugenia And while we're about it, when is the new phone exchange having its official opening, the one that will serve a third of the city, only a very few people know the official date, do you think you could find anybody at this border that knows that—it is September fourteenth. How many surburban lines are about to open in Moscow—four, with a total of forty-two stations, the original plan was for fifty, go and check that one, go on, you will find it is totally accurate. (*Watching them*) Tell me how could we possibly know these things—unless *he* was the Telephone Examiner of the Northern District.

A startled pause

(*Very forceful*) If what I tell you is true, which it is, you could be making a grave mistake comrade, for which you will be responsible. Don't you try to touch him again—I warn you, don't you maltreat him again in any way. (*Loudly*) And let us be on our way at once.

Eugenia faces them, the phone ringing in background. She turns and moves away

Guard 1 (*staring at her*) Madame . . .

Guard 2 (*tensely*) We've got another load to deal with in three minutes, it's coming in now.

Guard 1 (*staring at her*) I am making this decision for the wrong reasons and I will regret it, but for one moment, a moment that will no doubt seem absurd tomorrow (*staring at Eugenia*) you have convinced me, comrade, that he did indeed do that job. I have no idea why—look at the man! (*Pointing at Nikolai sitting in middle of carriage*) But you have. There still remains the diamonds. We will say we found them on another train. I will make no record of this incident. Nor of your departure, none will exist anywhere.

They both move

I don't advise you *ever* to try to come back.

They both exit

Silence

Nikolai (*calmly*) You truly can be said, without exaggeration, to be the Telephone Examiner of the Northern District.

Eugenia (*leaning her head against the side*) Not for long, not in a few minutes . . .

An ear-splitting screech, the sound of a locomotive backing up towards them, piercing sound of movement and violent braking that touches the pit of the stomach

Oh God—(*turning her head*)—I really don't want to go—how much you realize it now, when you can't turn back. (*Very quietly*) I wish something would happen to stop us going.

Nikolai Yes. I will have lost the race too, Eugenia, to be the first in my work, I have no money or resources now.

Eugenia You did it though. I know you did. We know we existed.

The crunch of the locomotive up close, the sounds are violent, wrenching

Nikolai (*with a slight smile*) Yes I can see myself bleating out in an omnibus in the middle of London, a hunched figure on the back seat, pointing at a ·

queue outside a talking motion picture house and saying I was the first to
do that!—and we started from much further behind.

Sasha (*moving*) I will write it up here Papa, I will leave it on the wall, a
record, there must be a record, the date . . . and what happened here.

The carriage begins to shake

Eugenia I wonder what this is going to be used for, (*quietly*) what's going to
be put in here.

Nikolai What we could have done Eugenia if we'd stayed . . .

Eugenia (*lying down as the carriage shakes, slowly curling up, trying to control
the emotions*) I know—I know that.

Nikolai There was a great deal more to be done.

Pause. The loud noise of the train is heard

God knows what's on the track. What already has been disposed of—
we're crunching over, passing over it as we move.

A loud violent noise

Eugenia (*looking round the carriage*) People going to be herded in here by
the hundred.

Sasha (*trying to write with a knife on the woodwork*) I can't make it write . . .
(*Loudly*) Oh, God, I can't make it write.

Nikolai (*quietly*) I'm just beginning to experience that tearing at the insides,
Eugenia, that feeling cutting through one . . . of helplessness. It's much
colder suddenly, Eugenia.

Eugenia (*curled up, letting out a cry of anger*) I don't want to leave.

Nikolai No, my love.

*The Lights are fading fast as they disappear into darkness as the carriage
lights go out, loud noise of movement continues*

My God it's cold. This is the worst part, can you still see me, can you?
(*Louder*) Can you?

Eugenia Just. (*She is curled up as the carriage shakes*) Just . . . I don't want
to go Nikolai I (*loudly*) I don't . . . I don't want to leave . . .

The Lights fade to Black-out

CURTAIN

FURNITURE AND PROPERTY LIST

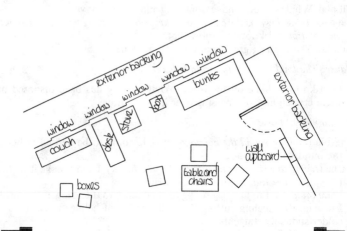

ACT I

SCENE 1

On stage: Couch
2 bunks. *On them:* dirty counterpanes, bedding, pillows
Stove
Table
4 chairs, some upturned
Wall cupboards
Desk
Chair
Several boxes. *Near one:* glass jar with onion in it
3 overhead fans (practical)
Bare floorboards with bloodstains
Dirt, straw, animal droppings on floor and beds
Curtains and blinds (closed) at windows

Off stage: 2 suitcases containing clothes, shoes, books **(Polya)**
Toy animal **(Sasha)**
Mahogany box containing pistols and packet of diamonds
Bag of money, ledger, pass and badge for Nikolai, 2 bread-rolls in pocket
(Verkoff)

SCENE 2

Set: Box of wood by stove
        Kettle, teapot, food, cups etc. on stove
        Blankets on couch, bunks
        Tidy suitcases under couch
        Bag of money, ledger, books on desk
        Pull blinds closed

Off stage: Baby carriage full of charred remains including newspaper **(Guard 2)**
        Bag of junk **(Guard 1)**

Personal: **Guards 1** and **2:** guns

SCENE 3

Set: Rugs on floor
        Table and 4 chairs C
        Screens around couch and desk **(Nikolai**'s area)
        Bags of money in desk drawer
        Pens, ink, papers, ledger on desk
        Unopened letters and telegrams in Nikolai's area and around carriage
        Blinds open
        Fans on
        Speaking apparatus on floor DR with long tube going out of carriage door
        Dishes in wall cupboard

SCENE 4

Set: Pistol for **Sasha**
        In boxes under bunks, around carraige and in wall cupboards: tablecloth,
          china, cutlery, silver candlesticks and candles, matches, glasses, bottle
          of wine, napkins, silver tray
        Speaking apparatus DL, tube lying on floor
        Ledger under bunk
        Polya's shawl on bunk
        In one of **Nikolai**'s cases: bulky camera

Off stage: Silver tray with pieces of meat **(Polya)**

Personal: **Verkoff:** envelope in pocket

ACT II

SCENE 1

Strike: Screens
        Dishes, cutlery, tablecloth etc. from table

Set: Tidy **Nikolai**'s belongings—equipment, papers on desk, speaking appara-
          tus and tube under desk
        Clothes-horses and lines with washing
        Kitchen utensils hanging up
        Piles of fruit and vegetables, other food stored
        Enamel bath, jug of water, towels DR

Eugenia's clothes on chair
Sasha's grey coat on chair
Sasha's fur coat on chair
Book for **Sasha**

Check: kettle, teapot, cups on stove

Personal: **Nikolai:** stick

SCENE 2

Strike: Washing, clothes-horses and lines
Bath, jug, towels
Nikolai's hat, coat, gloves, etc.
Sasha's grey coat

Set: Packing case C. *In it:* lenses, straw packing
Nickolai's sticks by desk
Papers, pens, equipment including hammer and knife on desk
Blinds closed

Personal: **Nikolai:** stick

SCENE 3

Set: Suitcases and bags half-packed
Boxes, clothes, possessions around carriage
Packing case in corner
Silk bag containing diamonds in package in desk
Pile of unopened letters in desk
Rugs rolled up
Blinds closed

Off stage: Clipboard, papers, pen **(Guard 1)**
Personal: **Guards 1** and **2:** guns

LIGHTING PLOT

Practical fittings required: 2 wall-lights on window wall, 3 overhead lights (with fans), light above door

Interior. A railway carriage. The same scene throughout

ACT I, Scene 1 Day

To open: Carriage in darkness, daylight outside

Cue 1	**Polya** pulls up blinds	(Page 1)
	As daylight shines through windows, increase general interior lighting	
Cue 2	**Nikolai:** ". . . nobody will dare touch us." *Black-out*	(Page 8)

ACT I, Scene 2 Night

To open: Black-out

Cue 3	When ready	(Page 8)
	Bring up interior lighting—all practicals on, light outside door	
Cue 4	**Sasha** turns one of the lights low *Decrease light*	(Page 13)
Cue 5	Door thrown open *Light streams in*	(Page 17)
Cue 6	Guard 1 exits, closing the door *Light decreases*	(Page 17)
Cue 7	**Nikolai:** ". . . till we hit the sea!" *Black-out*	(Page 17)

ACT I, Scene 3 Day

To open: General interior lighting—hot, sunny outside, fans on

Cue 8	**Polya** begins to sing, on her knees *Black-out*	(Page 24)

ACT I, Scene 4 Night

To open: Dim interior lighting, no practicals on, occasional flashes of gunfire outside in distance

Cue 9	As **Polya** lights candles *Increase lighting*	(Page 25)

Cue 10	Polya, Sasha, Eugenia and Verkoff take cover *White flash behind window*	(Page 29)
Cue 11	**Sasha:** "... I don't know Mama." *Light of flare from window*	(Page 32)
Cue 12	**Eugenia** snuffs out candles *Decrease lighting*	(Page 33)
Cue 13	**Eugenia:** "... we may be lucky." *Fade to black-out*	(Page 33)

ACT II, Scene 1 Day

To open: General interior lighting, winter daylight outside

Cue 14	**Nikolai:** "Polya—we must to work now." *Black-out*	(Page 42)

ACT II, Scene 2 Day

To open: Carriage in darkness, daylight outside

Cue 15	**Verkoff** opens blinds *Increase lighting*	(Page 43)
Cue 16	**Polya:** "Speak for yourself." *Black-out*	(Page 49)

ACT II, Scene 3 Night

To open: General interior lighting, all practicals on

Cue 17	**Polya** lifts blind to stare out of window *Passing light stabs through at them*	(Page 49)
Cue 18	**Nikolai:** "No, my love." *Snap out practicals*	(Page 63)
Cue 19	**Eugenia:** "I don't want to leave." *Fade to Black-out*	(Page 63)

EFFECTS PLOT

ACT I

Cue 1	**Nikolai:** "... to arrange partitions when I return." *Locomotive approaching in distance*	(Page 7)
Cue 2	**Nikolai:** "... without Polya's help, my dear." *Locomotive brakes very close and loud*	(Page 8)
Cue 3	**Sasha** (*excited*): "You want to take me?" *Locomotive hisses to a halt*	(Page 8)
Cue 4	**Nikolai:** "... nobody will dare touch us." *Locomotive moving through the night, changing into wail of locomotive, then screaming brakes, violently stuttering to a halt*	(Page 9)
Cue 5	As Scene 4 opens *Sporadic battle noise—distant grumbling gunfire, sniping, occasional field guns, shells falling*	(Page 24)
Cue 6	As **Polya** and **Eugenia** set table *Gunfire moves closer*	(Page 25)
Cue 7	**Eugenia:** "... where room service was." *Gunfire closer*	(Page 25)
Cue 8	**Verkoff:** "... are roaming the forest." *Gunfire*	(Page 26)
Cue 9	**Nikolai:** "... I am caged." *Gunfire, becoming closer*	(Page 26)
Cue 10	**Verkoff:** "... for saying less." *Shelling, becoming closer*	(Page 27)
Cue 11	**Polya:** "Just a little nice you know." *Very close gunfire*	(Page 28)
Cue 12	**Nikolai:** "... at the same time." *Shell breaks close to carriage*	(Page 29)
Cue 13	**Nikolai:** "... also in a forest." *Close sniper fire*	(Page 29)
Cue 14	**Nikolai:** "... nearer to civilization." *Loud whistle of shell directly above carriage*	(Page 29)
Cue 15	**Polya, Sasha, Eugenia** and **Verkoff** take cover *Shell explodes directly behind carriage*	(Page 29)
Cue 16	**Nikolai:** "... does not help." *Repeat Cue 14*	(Page 29)

Cue 17   **Nikolai:** "... reduced to a minimum."   (Page 29)
            Repeat Cue 15

Cue 18   **Nikolai:** "... with a false impression."   (Page 30)
            Gunfire further off

Cue 19   **Verkoff:** "... off his 'estate'!"   (Page 31)
            Distant gunfire

Cue 20   **Eugenia:** "... licking the ground."   (Page 32)
            Louder gunfire

Cue 21   **Sasha:** "... I don't know, Mama."   (Page 32)
            Flare goes up outside window

Cue 22   **Sasha:** "Nobody ... no-one."   (Page 32)
            Shell whistles and screams down, exploding behind carriage

Cue 23   **Eugenia:** "We both will."   (Page 32)
            Shells begin to fall

ACT II

Cue 24   As Scene 1 opens   (Page 34)
            Sounds of railway shunting yard; military band rehearsing—
            continue sporadically throughout scene

Cue 25   **Sasha:** "... the old foundations of the city ..."   (Page 35)
            Jarring notes of music outside

Cue 26   **Polya:** "... to keep me quiet——"   (Page 35)
            Sombre noise from band

Cue 27   **Polya** closes door after **Eugenia**   (Page 36)
            Burst from band

Cue 28   **Polya** seizes **Sasha**'s fur coat   (Page 38)
            Band plays

Cue 29   **Sasha** exits   (Page 39)
            Band rehearses

Cue 30   **Polya:** "... never crossed your mind."   (Page 41)
            Loud interrupted burst from band, with sudden drumming

Cue 31   **Nikolai:** "It is too technical for you."   (Page 42)
            Bell starts clanging in distance

Cue 32   **Nikolai:** "... help the deaf ..."   (Page 42)
            Band plays full, uninterrupted funeral march; more bells clang
            out

Cue 33   As Scene 2 opens   (Page 43)
            Train noise—clanking etc. over music and bells; loud noises, then
            silence

Cue 34   Black-out; as Scene 3 opens   (Page 49)
            Train noise—then braking, wrenching of metal; voices calling
            sporadically in distance, phones ringing, stopping, ringing
            again—continue intermittently

Cue 35   **Nikolai** (*calmly*): "I remember, yes."   (Page 49)
       Noise close by, outside

Cue 36   **Guard 1:** ". . . afford to make mistakes."   (Page 52)
       Telephone ringing in distance

Cue 37   **Nikolai:** "Yes."   (Page 55)
       Noise and movement outside

Cue 38   **Guard 2:** ". . . it never ever stops——"   (Page 55)
       Telephone and noise in distance—continue ringing

Cue 39   **Polya** appears framed in window   (Page 58)
       Sound of door being fastened from outside; telephone in distance

Cue 40   **Eugenia:** ". . . that's what happened."   (Page 58)
       Movement outside

Cue 41   **Eugenia:** "Yes I knew that."   (Page 59)
       Telephones in distance

Cue 42   **Eugenia:** ". . . on our way at once."   (Page 62)
       Telephones in distance

Cue 43   **Eugenia:** ". . . not in a few minutes . . ."   (Page 62)
       Ear-splitting screech as locomotive backs up, with piercing sound
       of movement and violent braking

Cue 44   **Eugenia:** "We know we existed."   (Page 62)
       Crunch of locomotive up close, violent, wrenching sounds

Cue 45   **Sasha:** ". . . and what happened here."   (Page 63)
       Carriage begins to shake. Loud train noises, continuing

Cue 46   **Nickolai:** ". . . passing over it as we move."   (Page 63)
       Loud violent noise; continue with carriage shaking and noise of
       movement until CURTAIN

MADE AND PRINTED IN GREAT BRITAIN BY
LATIMER TREND & COMPANY LTD PLYMOUTH
MADE IN ENGLAND